# Vegan Passport

## Fifth edition



Based on the original idea by Louise Wallis

First edition published July 1996

Second edition published June 2005

Third edition published February 2010

Fourth edition published November 2013

Fifth edition published July 2016



ISBN 978-0-9935425-0-3

Printed on recycled paper by SEEprint

Cover design – www.adamduncan.com

"If all else fails" illustrations by Adam Duncan

Published by The Vegan Society, Donald Watson House, 21 Hylton Street, Hockley, Birmingham, B18 6HJ, United Kingdom

All translations are believed to be accurate and are printed in good faith. The Vegan Society cannot accept liability for the consequences of any error in translation.

# Contents

## HOW TO USE THIS BOOK

When visiting a restaurant, show your waiter/waitress the relevant page of this book, and ask him/her to read it. Do not attempt to pronounce the text yourself! If you are invited to a private home for a meal, show your host/hostess the relevant page well in advance. If booking a hotel by post or email, send a copy of the relevant page. Please note that several languages may be used in the place you are visiting, so you may be able to offer the reader a choice of languages. See the index.

## COMMENT UTILISER CE PASSEPORT

Au restaurant, montrez la page correspondante à votre serveur/serveuse et demandez-lui de la lire. N'essayez pas de prononcer vous-même le texte! Si vous êtes invité(e) à déjeuner ou à diner chez les particuliers, montrez bien à l'avance la page correspondante à votre hôte. Si vous réservez un hôtel par correspondance ou par courrier électronique, envoyez une copie de la page correspondante. Notez que plusieurs langues peuvent être utilisées sur le lieu de votre visite, donc vous pouvez laisser le choix à votre interlocuteur en lui proposant les différentes langues. Voir l'index.

## COMO USAR ESTE LIVRO

Quando for a um restaurante, mostre ao empregado/à empregada de mesa a página apropriada deste livro e peça-lhes que a leiam. Não tente ser você a pronunciar as palavras do texto! Se o/a convidarem para uma refeição numa casa particular, mostre a página apropriada à pessoa que o/a vai receber, com bastante antecedência. Se fizer uma reserva de hotel por correio normal ou por correio electrónico, envie uma cópia da página apropriada. Por favor note que podem usar-se várias línguas no lugar que está a visitar, podendo assim oferecer ao leitor uma escolha de línguas. Consulte o índice.

## HINWEISE ZUR BENUTZUNG DIESES BUCHS

Beim Restaurantbesuch bitten Sie den Kellner bzw. die Kellnerin, die entsprechende Seite dieses Buches zu lesen. (Der Aussprache wegen ist dies immer besser als der Versuch, den Text vorzulesen.) Bei privaten Einladungen oder einer Hotelbuchung können Sie auch schon im Voraus eine Kopie der jeweiligen Seite überreichen bzw. verschicken. In mehrsprachigen Ländern bietet es sich an, die Seiten mehrerer Sprachen zu verwenden. (Siehe Index.)

## CÓMO USAR ESTE LIBRO

Cuando vaya a comer a un restaurante enseñe al camerero/a la camarera la página pertinente de este libro y pídale que la lea. ¡No trate de pronunciar el texto usted mismo! Si le invitan a comer en una casa particular asegúrese que sus anfitriones hayan leído con antelación la página pertinente. Si hace una reserva de hotel por correo envíeles una copia del texto. Tenga en cuenta que pueden hablar varias lenguas en el lugar que usted visite y debe dejar al lector elegir el idioma más pertinente. Ver el índice.

## КАК ВОСПОЛЬЗОВАТЬСЯ ЭТОЙ КНИГОЙ

При посещении ресторана покажите официанту / официантке соответствующую страницу в книге и попросите прочитать текст. Не пытайтесь сами произнести этот текст! Если вас пригласили в гости на угощение, заранее покажите хозяину или хозяйке соответствующую страницу. При бронировании гостиницы по обычной или электронной почте, пошлите копию соответствующей страницы. Пожалуйста, заметьте, что в месте вашего посещения могут использоваться несколько языков, поэтому вы можете предложить человеку, который будет читать текст, на выбор несколько языков, на которых написан текст. Смотрите указателя.

# List of languages

PLEASE READ THIS

## I am a vegan / We are vegans

As a vegan we do not eat anything of animal origin.

**So we do not eat:** meat, poultry (including chicken), fish, shellfish, or any other animal product such as eggs, milk or any dairy products, honey or gelatin.

**But we do eat:** all vegetables and fruits, rice, egg-free pasta and noodles, beans, mushrooms, nuts and seeds, cereals and grains.

**To make a vegan meal:** replace animal fat with vegetable oil or vegetable margarine, use vegetable stock in soups and sauces, check all ingredients for any animal products, and think creatively!

Please, can you provide a meal which meets our requirements?

THANK YOU VERY MUCH

# Afrikaans

LEES ASSEBLIEF DIE VOLGENDE

**Ek is 'n veganis / Ons is veganiste**

As 'n veganis eet ons niks wat van dierlike oorsprong is nie.

**Ons eet dus nie:** vleis, pluimvee (insluitend hoender), vis, skulpvis of enige ander diereproduk soos eiers, melk of enige suiwelprodukte, heuning of gelatien nie.

**Maar ons eet wel:** alle groente en vrugte, rys, eiervrye pasta en noedels, bone, sampioene, neute en sade, graankosse en graanprodukte.

**Om 'n veganiese maaltyd te maak:** Vervang dierevet met groenteolie of groente margarien, gebruik groente aftreksel in soppe en souse, kontroleer alle bestanddele vir enige diereprodukte en dink kreatief!

**Kan u asseblief 'n maaltyd verskaf wat aan ons behoeftes voldoen?**

BAIE DANKIE

# Albanian Shqip

JU LUTEMI, LEXOJENI

**Unë jam vegan / Ne jemi veganë**

Si veganë, ne nuk hamë ushqime me origjinë shtazore.

**Kësisoj nuk hamë:** mish, shpesë (duke përfshirë pulat), peshk, butakë ose produkte të tjera shtazore si vezët, qumështi apo bulmet tjetër, mjalti apo xhelatina.

**Por ne hamë:** të gjitha perimet dhe frutat, orizin, makaronat pa përmbajtje veze, bishtajoret, kërpudhat, frutat e thata, farat dhe drithërat.

**Për të përgatitur një vakt vegan:** zëvendësoni yndyrën shtazore me vaj vegjetal ose margarinë vegjetale, përdorni bazë perimesh te supat dhe salcat, kontrolloni të gjithë përbërësit për produkte shtazore dhe mendoni në mënyrë krijuese!

**Ju lutemi, a mund të na ofroni një vakt që plotëson kërkesat tona?**

**JU FALEMINDERIT SHUMË**

## Amharic                                                    አማርኛ

እባክዎን ይህንን መልእክት ያንብቡት

**እኔ አትክትል ተመጋቢ ነኝ / እኛ አትክትል ተመጋቢዎች ነን**

አትክልት ተጠቃሚዎች ስለሆንን ምንም አይነት የእንስሳት ተዋፅኦ አንመገብም

**ስለዚህ የማንመገባቸዉ ምግቦች የሚከተሉት ናቸዉ** -ስጋ፣ለእንቁላልና ስጋ የሚሆኑ ለማዳ ወፎች (ዶሮንም ያጠቃልላል)፣አሳ፣ጠንካራ ሽፋን ያለዉ አሳ፣እንዲሁም ማንኛዉም ለምግብነት የሚሆኑ የእንስሳት ዉጤቶች ይህም ማለት እንቁላል፣ወተትና ማንኛዉም የወተት ተዋፅኦ፣ማርና የሚያጣብቅ ምግብ

**ነገር ግን የሚከተሉትን ምግቦች እንመገባለን**--ሁሉም አይነት አትክልቶችና ፍራፍሬዎች፣ሩዝ፣በእንቁላል ያልተሰራ ፓስታና ኑድልስ፣ባቄላ፣መሽሩም፣የቅባት እህሎች፣ጥራጥሬና የእህል ዘር

**ለአትክልት ተመጋቢዎች ምግብ ለመስራት**--የእንስሳትን ዘይት በአትክልት ዘይት ወይም በአትክልት ማርጋሪን መተካት፣በሾርባና በመረቅ ዉስጥ የአትክልት ዉጤቶችን መጠቀም፣የእንስሳት ተዋፅኦ ምርቶች መኖራቸዉን ቼክ በማድረግ  የተሻለ አዲስ ሃሳብ ያቅርቡ!

**እባክዎ ከላይ የገለፅናቸዉን  አስፈላጊ መስፈርቶች በማሟላት ምግብ ሊዘጋጁልን ይችላሉ?**

ስለትብብርዎ እናመሰግናለን!

يرجى قراءة ما يلي

أنا نباتي / نحن نباتيون.

بصفتنا نباتيين، فنحن لا نأكل أي شيء من أصل حيواني.

لذلك نحن لا نأكل: اللحوم أو الدواجن (بما في ذلك الدجاج) أو الأسماك أو المحار أو أي منتج حيواني آخر مثل البيض أو الحليب أو أي من منتجات

الألبان أو العسل أو الجيلاتين.

ولكننا نأكل: جميع الخضروات والفواكه والأرز، والمعكرونة والشعرية الخالية من البيض، والفاصوليا، والفطر، والمكسرات والبذور والحبوب.

لتحضير وجبة نباتية: استبدل الدهون الحيوانية بالزيت النباتي أو السمن النباتي ، استخدم المرق النباتي في الشوربة والصلصات، وتحقق من جميع المكونات لأي من المنتجات الحيوانية، وفكر بأسلوب خلاق!

من فضلك، هل يمكنك تقديم وجبة تلبي متطلباتنا؟

شكرا جزيلا

IRAKURRI HAU

**Beganoa naiz / Beganoak gara**

Begano gisa ez dugu animalietatik datorren ezer jaten.

**Beraz ez ditugu jaten:** haragia, hegaztiak (oilaskoa barne), arraina, itsaskiak edo animalietatik datorren edozein produktu, hala nola, arrautzak, esnea edo esnekiak, eztia edo gelatina.

**Baina honako hauek jaten ditugu:** barazki eta fruta guztiak, arroza, arrautzarik gabe egindako pasta eta noodle-ak, lekaleak, onddoak, fruitu lehorrak eta haziak, zerealak eta aleak.

**Janari beganoa jateko:** Ordezkatu animalien koipea olio begetalarekin edo margarina begetalarekin, erabili barazkiekin egindako saldak eta saltsak zopetan, egiaztatu animalietatik datozen produktuen osagai guztiak eta atera zure sormena!

**Faborez, emango diguzu gure eskakizunak betetzen dituen janariren bat?**

MILA ESKER

MUKWAI BELENGENI IFI

**Nshilya inama / Tatulya Inama**

Pamo nga abashilya inama tatulya fyonse fye ifipangwa ukufuma ku nama.

**Ifwe kanshi tatulya ifi:** umunani wa nama, ifyuni (ukubikapo na inkoko), isabi, isabi lyamu fipapa, nangu fyonse fye ifipangwa ku nama pamo nga amani, umukaka nangu fyonse ifipangwa ku mukaka, ubuci elyo na gelatini.

**Nomba ifyo tulya nifi:** imisalu yonse ne fisabo, umupunga, utubulungwa twa mukate umushaba umukaka, cilemba, ubowa elyo na inseke mumisango ya shiko.

**Pakupekanya ifyakulya fya bashilya inama:** munshita yakubomfya amafuta yanama bomfyeni amafuta yamisalu nangu ishiba lya misalu, mumuto namo bomfyeni ishiba namafuta ya misalu, ceceteni nokumona fyonse ifingasanshiwamo ifya nama, tontonkanyenipo inshila nashimbi isho mwingafiwamishamo!

**Mukwai, bengatupekanishishako icakulya iciyene ne mifwaile yesu?**

TWATASHA NGANSHI MUKWAI

Bengali    বাংলা

**অনুগ্রহ করে এটি পড়ুন আমি/আমরা ভেজান।**

ভেজান হিসাবে আমরা প্রাণীজাত কিছুই খাই না।

**সে কারনে আমরা খাই না:** মাংস, পোলট্রি (মুরগি সহ), মাছ, শেলফিস বা চিংড়ি জাতীয় মাছ, অথবা অন্য কোন প্রাণীজ উৎসের পণ্য যেমন ডিম, দুধ বা দুগ্ধজাত কোনো পণ্য , মধু বা জেলাটিন।

**তবে আমরা খাই:** সকল শাক-সবজি ও ফলমূল, চাল, ডিমহীন পাস্তা এবং নুডলস, শুটি, মাশরুম, বাদাম এবং বীজ, শস্যাদি এবং ডাল।

**একটি ভেজান খাদ্য তৈরিতে:** উদ্ভিজ্জ তেল দিয়ে প্রাণীজ চর্বি প্রতিস্থাপন অথবা উদ্ভিজ্জ মার্জারিন ব্যবহার করুন, স্যুপ তৈরিতে উদ্ভিজ্জ স্টক ও সস ব্যবহার করুন, সকল উপাদানে কোন প্রানীজ পণ্যের উপস্থিতি আছে কিনা তা পরখ করুন এবং সৃজনশীলতা দিয়ে ভাবুন।

**দয়া করে এমন একটি খাবার কি দিতে পারেন যা আমাদের প্রয়োজনীয়তা পূরণ করতে পারে?**

**অনেক ধন্যবাদ**

## Bulgarian **Български**

МОЛЯ, ПРОЧЕТЕТЕ

**Аз съм веган/Ние сме вегани**

Като вегани, ние не ядем нищо, което е с животински произвоход.

**Което значи, че не ядем:** месо, месо от домашни птици (включително и пилешко), риба, ракообразни или каквито и да е други животински продукти, като яйца, мляко или млечни продукти, мед или желатин.

**Но ядем:** всякакви плодове и зеленчуци, орис, макаронени изделия и юфка без съдържание на яйца, бобови, гъби, ядки и семена, зърнени култури и зърнени храни.

**За да приготвите веганско ястие:** заменете животинската мазнина с растително масло или растителен маргарин, използвайте зеленчуков бульон в супите и сосовете, проверете всички съставки за съдържание на животински продукти и бъдете креативни!

**Можете ли да ни предоставите ястие, което отговаря на нашите изисквания?**

**МНОГО ВИ БЛАГОДАРИМ**

# Burmese

# မြန်မာ

ကျေးဇူးပြုပြီး ဖတ်ပါ

**ကျွန်တော် သတ်သတ်လွတ်သမားတစ်ယောက်ပါ/ ကျွန်ုပ်တို့ သတ်သတ်လွတ်သမားတွေပါ**

သတ်သတ်သမားဖြစ်တဲ့အတွက် အသားတွေ တိရစ္ဆာန်မှရတဲ့အစားအစာမှန်သမျှ မစားကြပါဘူး။

**ဒါကြောင့် ကျွန်ုပ်တို့မစားတဲ့အစားအစာတွေကတော့** အသား၊ ဥစား အသားစားအတွက်မွေးမြူထားသော တိရစ္ဆာန်များ (ကြက်အပါအဝင်)၊ ငါး၊ အကြေးခွံပါသောငါး၊ ဥနှင့်နို့ကဲ့သို့သော တိရစ္ဆာန်မှ ရသော အစားအစာများ သို့မဟုတ် နို့ထွက်ပစ္စည်းများ၊ ပျားရည်နှင့် တိရစ္ဆာန်အရေခွံနှင့်အရိုးကိုပြုတ်ပြီး ပြုလုပ်ထားသော ပျစ်ခဲ့သည့် ဂျယ်လီများ စသည်တို့ကို ကျွန်ုပ်တို့မစားပါ။

**ကျွန်ုပ်တို့စားသည့်အစားအစာကတော့** အသီးအရွက်နှင့် သီးနှံအားလုံး၊ ဆန်၊ ကြက်ဥမပါသော အီတလီခေါက်ဆွဲခြောက် နှင့် ခေါက်ဆွဲများ၊ ပဲအမျိုး၊ မှို အစေ့အဆံများ၊ ကောက်ပဲသီးနှံနှင့် ဂျုံးစသည် တို့ဖြစ်တယ်။

**သတ်သတ်လွတ်အစားအစာချက်ပြုတ်ရန်အတွ**က် တိရစ္ဆာန်အဆီအစား အသီးအရွက်အဆီ သို့မဟုတ် မာဂျရင်းတို့ဖြင့် အစားထိုးအသုံးပြုပါ။ ဟင်းချိုနှင့် ဆော့ထဲတွင် အသီးအရွက်ထွက်ကုန်များကို အသုံးပြုပါ၊ တိရစ္ဆာန်မှ ရရှိသော အစားအသောက်များမပါဝင်အောင် သတိထားပြီး ဆန်းသစ်တီထွင်သော နည်းလမ်းများ စဉ်းစားပြီး ပြုလုပ်ပေးပါ။

**ကျေးဇူးပြုပြီး ကျွန်တို့လိုအပ်ချက်နဲ့ကိုက်ညီတဲ့ အစားအသောက်များကို ခင်ဗျားပြုလုပ်ပေးနိုင်ပါသလား။**

**ကျေးဇူးအများကြီးတင်ပါတယ်။**

# Catalan

SI US PLAU, LLEGEIXI AIXÒ

**Sóc vegetarià / Som vegetarians**

Com a vegetarians, no mengem res d'origen animal.

**Així, no mengem:** Carn, aviram (inclòs el pollastre), peix, marisc, o qualsevol altre producte animal com ara ous, llet o qualssevol productes lactis, mel o gelatina.

**Però mengem:** Totes les verdures i fruites, arròs, pasta sense ou, fideus, mongetes, xampinyons, nous, llavors, cereals i grans.

**Per preparar un àpat vegetarià:** Substitueixi el greix animal per l'oli vegetal o la margarina vegetal, utilitzi el brou de verdures en les sopes i salses, comprovi tots els ingredients per evitar els productes animals i pensi creativament!

**Si us plau, pot proporcionar un àpat en harmonia amb els nostres requisits?**

MOLTES MERCÈS

# Chinese (Simplified) 简体中文

请阅读这篇短文

**我是一个素食主义者 / 我们是素食主义者**

作为素食主义者，我们不吃有任何动物成分的食物。

**所以我们不吃：**肉类，家禽（包括鸡），鱼类，有壳的水生动物或任何其他动物产品，如鸡蛋，牛奶或任何乳制品，蜂蜜或动物胶。

**但我们吃：**所有的蔬菜和水果，大米，不含鸡蛋的意大利面食和面条，豆类，蘑菇，坚果和种子，谷物和谷粮。

**怎样做素餐：**用植物油或植物黄油替代动物脂肪油，在汤和酱料中使用蔬菜高汤，检查所有的作料中是否含有任何动物成分，发挥想象力进行创造性的思考！

**请您提供一份符合我们要求的膳食，好吗？**

**非常感谢**

# Chinese (Traditional) 繁體中文

請閱讀這篇短文

**我是一個素食主義者 / 我們是素食主義者**

作為素食主義者，我們不吃有任何動物成分的食物。

**所以我們不吃：**肉類，家禽（包括雞），魚類，有殼的水生動物或任何其他動物產品，　如雞蛋，牛奶或任何乳製品，蜂蜜或動物膠。

**但我們吃：**所有的蔬菜和水果，大米，不含雞蛋的意大利麵食和麵條，豆類，蘑菇，堅果和種子，穀物和谷糧。

**怎樣做素餐：**用植物油或植物黃油替代動物脂肪油，在湯和醬料使用蔬菜高湯，檢查所有的作料中是否含有任何動物成分，發揮想象力進行創造性的思考！

**請您提供一份符合我們要求的膳食，好嗎？**

**非常感謝**

## Croatian Hrvatski

MOLIMO, PROČITAJTE OVO

**Ja sam vegan/Mi smo vegani**

Kao vegani, ne jedemo ništa životinjskog podrijetla.

**Tako ne jedemo:** meso, perad (uključujući piletinu), ribu, školjkaše ili bilo kakve druge životinjske proizvode kao jaja, mlijeko i druge mliječne proizvode, med i želatinu.

**Ali jedemo:** svo povrće i voće, rižu, tjesteninu i rezance bez jaja, grahorice, gljive, orašaste proizvode, sjemenke i žitarice.

**Kako napraviti veganski obrok:** zamijenite životinjsku mast s biljnim uljem ili biljnim margarinom, upotrijebite povrtni temeljac u juhama i umacima, provjerite sve sastojke sadrže li životinjske proizvode i razmišljajte kreativno!

**Možete li nam, molimo vas, dati obrok koji zadovoljava naše potrebe?**

PUNO HVALA

# Czech Čeština

PŘEČTĚTE SI TO, PROSÍM

**Jsem vegán/ vegánka / Jsme vegáni**

Jako vegáni nejíme nic, co je živočišného původu.

**Znamená to, že nejíme:** maso, drůbež (včetně kuřecího masa), ryby, korýše, ani žádné jiné živočišné produkty, jako například vejce, mléko anebo mléčné výrobky, med anebo želatinu.

**Jíme ale:** všechnu zeleninu a ovoce, rýži, bezvaječné těstoviny a nudle, luštěniny, houby, ořechy a semínka, obiloviny a zrna.

**Jak připravit veganské jídlo:** nahraďte živočišné tuky rostlinným olejem anebo rostlinným margarínem, do polévek a omáček použijte zeleninový bujon, zkontrolujte všechny ingredience, jestli neobsahují živočišné produkty a myslete tvořivě!

**Můžete nám, prosím, poskytnout jídlo, které splňuje naše požadavky?**

MOCKRÁT DĚKUJEME!

# Danish Dansk

LÆS VENLIGST DETTE

**Jeg er veganer / Vi er veganere**

Som veganer spiser vi ikke noget, som kommer fra dyr.

**Derfor spiser vi ikke:** Kød, fjerkræ (inklusiv kylling), fisk, skalddyr eller andre former for animalske produkter så som æg, mælk eller andre mælkeprodukter, honning eller gelatine.

**Til gengæld spiser vi gerne:** Alle former for grønsager og frugt, ris, pasta og nudler uden æg, bønner, svampe, nødder og frø, morgencerealier og korn.

**For at lave et vegansk måltid:** Erstat animalsk fedt med vegetabilske olier eller vegetabilsk margarine, benyt grønsagsfond i supper og saucer, check alle ingredienser for enhver form for animalske produkter og tænk kreativt!

**Kan I venligst servere et måltid, som lever op til vores behov?**

MANGE TAK

LEES DIT A.U.B.

**Ik ben veganist/wij zijn veganisten**

Een veganist eet geen enkel product van dierlijke oorsprong.

**Wij eten dus geen:** vlees, gevogelte (inclusief kip), vis, schaaldieren of andere dierlijke producten zoals eieren, melk of zuivel, honing of gelatine.

**Maar we eten wel:** alle groenten en fruit, rijst, pasta en noedels vrij van eieren, bonen, paddenstoelen, noten, zaden en graanproducten.

**Om een veganistische maaltijd klaar te maken:** vervang dierlijk vet met plantaardige olie of plantaardige margarine, gebruik groentenbouillon in soepen en sauzen, check alle ingrediënten op dierlijke producten en wees creatief!

**Kunt u voor ons een maaltijd klaarmaken die aan deze wensen voldoet?**

HARTELIJK BEDANKT

Esperanto **Angla**

BONVOLU LEGI TION

**Mi estas vegano / Ni estas veganoj**

Kiel veganoj ni ne manĝas ion ajn de animala deveno.

**Do ni ne manĝas:** viandon, birdaĵon (inkluzive de kokaĵo), fiŝojn, marfruktojn aŭ ajnajn aliajn animalajn produktojn kiel ovoj, lakto kaj laktoproduktoj, mielo kaj gelateno.

**Sed ni manĝas:** ĉiujn legomojn kaj fruktojn, rizon, senovajn pastaĵojn kaj nudelojn, fazeolojn, fungojn, nuksojn kaj semojn, grenojn kaj grajnojn.

**Por fari veganan manĝaĵon:** Anstataŭigu animalan grason per vegetala oleo aŭ margarino, en supoj kaj saŭcoj uzu vegetalan buljonon, kontrolu ĉiujn ingrediencojn, ĉu ili ne enhavas iajn animalaĵojn, kaj pensu kreeme!

**Ĉu vi povas bonvolu havigi manĝaĵon, kiu plenumas niajn kondiĉojn?**

DANKEGON

PALUN LUGEGE SEDA

**Ma olen vegan / Me oleme veganid**

Veganitena ei söö me midagi, millel on loomne päritolu.

**Seega me ei söö:** liha, linnuliha (kaasa arvatud kanaliha), kala, koorikloomi ega mingit muud loomset toodet nagu mune, piima ega mingisuguseid piimatooteid, mett ega želatiini.

**Aga me sööme:** kõiki juurvilju ja puuvilju, riisi, munavaba pastat ja nuudleid, ube, seeni, pähkleid ja seemneid, putru ja teraviljatooteid.

**Veganeine valmistamiseks:** asendage loomne rasv taimeõli või margariiniga, kasutage suppides ja kastmetes taimepuljongit, kontrollige igasuguste loomsete toodete leidmiseks kõiki koostisosi ja mõtelge loovalt!

**Kas te võite meile anda meie nõuetele vastavat sööki?**

SUUR TÄNU!

## Finnish Suomi

LUE TÄMÄ

**Olen vegaani / Olemme vegaaneja**

Koska olemme vegaaneja, emme syö mitään, mikä on lähtöisin eläimestä.

**Joten emme syö seuraavia:** liha, siipikarja (mukaan lukien kana), kala, simpukka tai muut eläinkunnan tuotteet, kuten kananmunat, maito tai maitotaloustuotteet, hunaja tai gelatiini.

**Mutta syömme seuraavia:** kaikki kasvikset ja hedelmät, riisi, kananmunia sisältämätön pasta ja nuudelit, pavut, sienet, pähkinät ja siemenet, viljatuotteet ja murot.

**Vegaaniaterian valmistaminen:** korvaa eläinrasvat kasvisöljyllä tai margariinilla, käytä kasvisliemiä keitoissa ja kastikkeissa, tarkista, että missään valmistusaineissa ei ole eläinkunnan tuotteita, ja ole luova!

**Voitteko tarjota meille aterian, joka täyttää vaatimuksemme?**

KIITOS ERITTÄIN PALJON

# French Français

VEUILLEZ LIRE CECI

**Je suis végétalien(ne) / Nous sommes végétaliens**

En tant que végétaliens, nous ne mangeons rien d'origine animale.

**Donc nous ne mangeons pas:** la viande, la volaille (y compris le poulet), les poissons, les crustacés et tout autre produit d'origine animale tel que les œufs, le lait ou tous les produits laitiers, le miel ou la gélatine.

**Mais nous mangeons:** tous les légumes et les fruits, le riz, les pâtes sans œufs, les nouilles, les haricots, les champignons, les noix et les graines, les céréales et les fibres.

**Pour préparer un repas végétalien:** remplacer la matière grasse animale par de l'huile végétale ou de la margarine végétale, utiliser du bouillon de légumes dans les soupes et les sauces, contrôler tous les ingrédients pour vérifier s'ils contiennent des produits d'origine animale, et penser de manière créative !

**Pouvez-vous, s'il vous plaît, nous offrir un repas qui répond à nos exigences alimentaires?**

MERCI BEAUCOUP

## Galician Galego

Lea isto, por favor

**Son vegano/somos veganos**

Os veganos non consumimos nada que teña orixe animal.

**Polo tanto, non comemos:** carne de vacún, carne de ave (incluíndo o polo), pescado, marisco, nin calquera outro alimento de orixe animal, como os ovos, o leite, o resto de produtos lácteos, a mel e a xelatina.

**Porén, si comemos:** todo tipo de froitas e verduras, arroz, pasta que non estea feita con ovo, legumes, setas, froitos secos, cereais e grans.

**Para preparar unha comida vegana:** substitúa a graxa animal por aceite ou margarina vexetal, use caldo vexetal nas sopas e salsas, comprobe que ningún ingrediente é de orixe animal e... sexa creativo!

**Pode ofrecernos unha comida que cumpra as nosas necesidades?**

MOITAS GRAZAS

# German / Deutsch

BITTE LESEN

## Ich lebe vegan / Wir leben vegan

Als Veganer essen wir nichts tierischen Ursprungs.

**Das essen wir nicht:**
Fleisch, Geflügel (Hühnchen mit inbegriffen), Fisch, Meeresfrüchte oder tierische Produkte wie Eier, Milch, Milchprodukte, Honig oder Gelatine.

**Das essen wir:**
Jede Gemüse- und Fruchtart, Reis, Nudeln ohne Ei, Bohnen, Pilze, Nüsse und Samen, Getreide und Körner.

**Wie bereitet man ein veganes Gericht zu?**
Ersetzen Sie tierisches Fett durch pflanzliches Öl oder pflanzliche Margarine. Verwenden Sie Pflanzenbrühe für Suppen und Soßen. Überprüfen Sie alle Inhaltsstoffe auf tierische Produkte und: Seien Sie kreativ!

**Würden Sie uns bitte ein Gericht zubereiten, das unseren Anforderungen entspricht?**

VIELEN DANK

**ΠΑΡΑΚΑΛΕΙΣΤΕ ΝΑ ΔΙΑΒΑΣΕΤΕ ΤΟ ΠΑΡΟΝ**

**Είμαι χορτοφάγος / Είμαστε χορτοφάγοι**

Ως χορτοφάγοι δεν τρώμε τίποτα ζωικής προέλευσης.

**Επομένως δεν τρώμε:** κρέας, πουλερικά (συμπεριλαμβανομένου και του κοτόπουλου), ψάρι, οστρακοειδή, ή οποιοδήποτε άλλο ζωικό προϊόν όπως για παράδειγμα αυγά, γάλα ή οποιοδήποτε άλλο γαλακτοκομικό προϊόν, μέλι ή ζελατίνη.

**Τρώμε όμως:** όλα τα λαχανικά και τα φρούτα, ρύζι, ζυμαρικά και noodles χωρίς αυγό, φασόλια, μανιτάρια, ξηροί καρποί και σπόροι, δημητριακά και σιτηρά.

**Πώς να ετοιμάσετε ένα γεύμα για χορτοφάγους:** αντικαταστήστε το ζωικό λίπος με φυτικό λάδι ή φυτική μαργαρίνη, χρησιμοποιήστε κύβους λαχανικών στις σούπες και τις σάλτσες, ελέγξτε όλα τα συστατικά για τυχόν ζωικά προϊόντα και αφήστε τη φαντασία σας να δημιουργήσει!

**Παρακαλώ μπορείτε να μας παρέχετε ένα γεύμα που να ικανοποιεί τις απαιτήσεις μας;**

**ΣΑΣ ΕΥΧΑΡΙΣΤΟΥΜΕ ΠΟΛΥ**

કૃપા કરી આ વાંચો

**હું વીગન છું / અમે વીગન છીએ**

**(વીગન - પ્રાણી દ્વારા ઉત્પાદિત કોઇપણ ખોરાક ન ખાનાર)**

વીગન તરીકે અમે પ્રાણી દ્વારા ઉત્પાદિત કોઈપણ વસ્તુ ખાતા નથી.

**તેથી અમે આ નથી ખાતા:** માંસ, મરઘાં–બતકાં (ચિકન સહિત), માછલી, શેલફીશ, અથવા અન્ય કોઇ પ્રાણી ઉત્પાદનો જેમ કે ઇંડા, દૂધ અથવા કોઈપણ ડેરી ઉત્પાદન, મધ અથવા જીલેટીન.

**પરંતુ અમે ખાઇએ છીએ:** તમામ શાકભાજી અને ફળો, ચોખા, ઇંડા વગરના પાસ્તા અને નૂડલ્સ, કઠોળ, મશરૂમ, સૂકા ફળ અને મેવો, અનાજ અને ધાન.

**વીગન ખોરાક બનાવવા માટે:** પશુની ચરબીને બદલે વેજીટેબલ તેલ અથવા વેજીટેબલ માર્ગરિનનો ઉપયોગ કરો, સૂપ અને સોસમાં વેજીટેબલ સ્ટોકનો ઉપયોગ કરો, કોઈપણ પ્રાણી ઉત્પાદન ન હોય તે માટે તમામ સામગ્રી તપાસો, અને સર્જનાત્મક વિચારો!

**શું તમે અમારી જરૂરીયાત મુજબનું ભોજન આપી શકશો?**

**તમારો ખૂબ ખૂબ આભાર**

KARANTA WANNAN

**Ni ba na cin nama / Mu ba ma cin nama**

Yanayinmu shi ne mu ba ruwanmu da cin naman duk wata dabba.

**Don haka ba ma cin:** nama, dabbobi ko na tsuntsaye (har da na kaji), da kifi da dodon kodi, har ma da su kwai, da madara ko nono, da zuma, da kuma kitse.

**Amma kuma muna cin:** 'ya'yan itatuwa, da kayan marmari, da shinkafa, da taliya, da makaroni, da wake, da rumfar kwado da gyada da ridi dahatsi.

**Yadda za a shirya abincin wanda ba ya cin nama shi ne:** a maye gurbin kitsen dabbobi da man 'ya'yan itatuwa, a yi amfani da 'ya'yan itatuwa a cikin miya da kuma kwanon cin abinci, a kula da duk wani nau'in naman dabbobi kada, ya shiga cikin abincin!

**Don Allah, za ka iya samar mana da abinci irin wanda ya dace da mu?**

MUN GODE

# Hebrew

# עברית

נא לקרוא

**אני טבעוני/ אנחנו טבעונים**

כטבעוניים, אנחנו לא אוכלים דברי מאכל שמקורם מן החי.

**לכן אנחנו לא אוכלים:** בשר, עוף, דגים, פירות ים, או כל מוצר אחר מן החי כולל ביצים, חלב או מוצרי חלב, דבש או ג׳לטין.

**אבל אנחנו כן אוכלים:** כל הירקות והפירות, אורז, פסטה ואטריות ללא ביצים, שעועית, פטריות, אגוזים וגרעינים, ודגנים.

**להכין ארוחה טבעונית:** יש להחליף את השומן מן החי עם שומן צמחי או מרגרינה, להשתמש באבקת מרק פרווה למרקים ורטבים, לבדוק שכל המרכיבים חופשיים ממוצרים מן החי, ולחשוב ביצירתיות!

אנא, האם אתה יכול להכין ארוחה לפי דרישותינו?

**מודים לכם מאוד**

# Hindi

# हिन्दी

कृपया इसे पढें

**हम शाकाहारी हैं।**

शाकाहारी होने कारण हम जानवरों से बनी कोई चीज नहीं खाते।

**इस लिये हम यह चीजें नहीं खाते:** मास, (चूजे सहित) पक्षी मास, मछली, शेल्फिश, या जानवरों से बनी दूसरी चीजें जैसे कि अंडे, दूध या डेयरी उत्पाद, शहद जिलेटिन (सरेस)।

**परंतू हम ये चीजें खा लेते हैं:** सभ सब्जीयां व फल, चावल, अंडा रहत पास्ता व नूडलज, बीनज, मशरूमज, नट्स और सीडज, सीरियलज व दाने।

**शाकाहारी भोजन बनाने के लिये:** जानवरों की चरबी की जगह वेजीटेबल तेल या मार्जरीन का प्रयोग करें, सूप और चटनी के लिये वेजीटेबल स्टौक का प्रयोग करें, पूरी साम्ग्री को जानवरों के उत्पादों के लिये चैक करें और रचनात्म्क सोच अपनायें।

**क्या आप कुपया हमारी जरूरतें पूरी करने वाला भोजन प्रदान कर सकते हैं?**

**आप जी का बहुत बहुत धन्यावाद।**

# Hungarian Magyar

KÉREM OLVASSA EL

**Vegán vagyok / Vegánok vagyunk**

Vegánként nem fogyasztok/tunk semmilyen állati eredetű élelmiszert.

**Azaz nem fogyasztunk**: húst, szárnyasokat (csirkehúst is beleértve), halat, kagylót vagy bármilyen más állati eredetű terméket, úgymint tojást, tejet vagy tejterméket, mézet vagy zselatint.

**Fogyasztunk viszont:** mindenféle zöldséget és gyümölcsöt, rizst, tojásmentes száraz- vagy metélt tésztát, babokat, gombákat, olajos és más magvakat, gabonapelyheket és gabonaféléket.

**Vega étel elkészítésének módja**: az állati eredetű zsiradékot helyettesítsük növényi olajjal vagy margarinnal, használjunk zöldségkockát a levesek és szószok elkészítéséhez, ellenőrizzünk minden hozzávalót, nem tartalmaz-e nyomokban bármilyen állati eredetű összetevőt és használjuk a kreativitásunkat!

**Kaphatnánk olyan ételt, amely a fenti követelményeknek megfelel?**

NAGYON KÖSZÖNÖM / KÖSZÖNJÜK!

# Icelandic Íslenska

VINSAMLEGA LESIÐ

**Ég er vegan / við erum vegan**

Sem vegan borðum við engar dýraafurðir.

**Því borðum við ekki:** kjöt, fuglakjöt (þar á meðal kjúkling), fisk, skelfisk, eða aðrar dýraafurðir eins og egg, mjólk eða aðrar mjólkurvörur, hunang eða gelatín.

**En við borðum:** allt grænmeti og ávexti, hrísgrjón, pasta og núðlur án eggja, baunir, sveppi, hnetur og fræ, kornmeti og grjón.

**Til að búa til vegan máltíð:** Notið jurtaolíu eða jurtasmjörlíki í staðinn fyrir dýrafitu, notið grænmetiskraft í súpur og sósur, athugið hvort innihaldsefni innihaldi dýraafurðir og hugsið með skapandi hætti!

**Getur þú boðið upp á máltíð sem uppfyllir kröfur okkar?**

ÞAKKA ÞÉR KÆRLEGA FYRIR

BIKO GỤỌ NKE A

**Anaghị m eri anụ / Anyị anaghị eri anụ**

Dị ka onye anaghị eri anụ anyị anaghị eri ihe ọ bụla si n'anụ.

**Yabụ, anyị anaghị eri:** anụ, nnụnụ (gụnyere ọkụkọ), azụ, azụ okporoko, ma ọ bụ nri anụ ọ bụla ọzọ dịka akwa, mmiri ara ehi ma ọ bụ nri ọ bụla si n'ehi, mmanụ aṅwụ ma ọ bụ jelatịn.

**Mana anyị na eri:** akwụkwọ nri na mkpụrụ osisi niile, osikapa, pasta na enweghị akwa yana nudul, agwa, ero, mkpụrụ na mkpụrụ osisi, mkpụrụ ọka na.

**Ịme nri onye na anaghị eri anụ:** jiri mmanụ akwụkwọ nri ma ọ bụ majarịn akwụkwọ nri wee dochie abụba anụ, jiri nri akwụkwọ nri n'ofe yana sọs, lelee ngwa nri niile maka nri anụ ọ bụla, chee echiche!

**Biko, ị nwere ike ịnye nri zutere ihe ndị anyị chọrọ?**

DAALỤ NKE UKWUU

# Indonesian　Bahasa Indonesia

HARAP DIBACA

**Saya seorang vegan / Kami vegan**

Sebagai vegan, kami tidak mengonsumsi apa pun yang berasal dari hewan.

**Jadi kami tidak memakan:** daging, unggas (termasuk ayam), ikan, kerang-kerangan, atau produk hewan lainnya seperti telur, susu atau produk susu lainnya, madu atau gelatin.

**Namun, kami memakan:** semua sayuran dan buah, nasi, pasta dan mi bebas telur, kacang, jamur, kacang-kacangan dan biji-bijian, sereal, dan gandum.

**Untuk membuat hidangan vegan:** ganti lemak hewan dengan minyak nabati atau margarine nabati, gunakan kaldu sayuran dalam sup dan saus, cek bila semua bahan mengandung produk hewan, dan berpikirlah kreatif!

**Dapatkan Anda menyediakan hidangan sesuai dengan kebutuhan kami?**

TERIMA KASIH BANYAK

BHITHEAMAID FADA NUR COMAIN

NAN LEUGHADH SIBH SEO

**'S e veganach a tha annam / 'S e veganaich a tha annainn**

Chan ith veganach rud sam bith a chaidh a dhèanamh de bheathach.

**Chan ith sinn na leanas ri linn sin:** feòil, eunlaith (a' gabhail a-staigh circfheoil), iasg, maorach no stuth beathaich mar uighean, bainne no math na bà sam bith, mil no dealatain.

**Ach ithidh sinn na leanas:** lus is meas sam bith, rìs, pasta is nùdailean gun uighean ann, pònairean, balgain bhuachrach, cnòthan is sìl, gràn bhàrr is gràinnean.

**Nithear biadh veganach:** le bhith a' cur ola lusan no margarain lusan an àite geir bheathaichean, a' cleachdadh sùgh glasraich ann am brot no sabhs, a' sgrùdadh gach grìtheid ach a bheil bathar beathaich ann agus le bhith cruthachail!

**Am b' urrainn dhuibh biadh ullachadh dhuinn a bhios freagarrach dhuinn?**

MÒRAN TAING

LEGGERE ATTENTAMENTE

**Sono vegano / Siamo vegani**

Noi vegani non mangiamo nessun derivato di origine animale.

**Quindi non mangiamo:** carne rossa, carni bianche (pollo incluso), pesce, crostacei e molluschi o qualsiasi altro derivato animale come uova, latte e prodotti latteari, miele o gelatina.

**Ma mangiamo:** tutti la frutta e i vegetali, riso, tutti i tipi di pasta senza uovo, fagioli, funghi, noci, semi, cereali e granaglie.

**Preparare un pasto vegano:** Sostituite il grasso animale con dell'olio vegetale o della margarina, utilizzate brodo vegetale per zuppe o salse, controllate che tutti gli ingredienti non abbiano derivazione animale e siate creativi!

**Siete in grado di proporre un pasto che possa soddisfare le nostre esigenze?**

GRAZIE MILLE

# Japanese 日本語

こちらをお読みください

**私はヴィーガンです/私たちはヴィーガンです**

ヴィーガンである私たちは動物性由来の物は一切食べません。

**では私たちが食べない物：** お肉、家禽肉（鶏肉を含む）、魚、 貝類、または卵、牛乳や乳製品、蜂蜜もしくはゼラチン等、他全ての動物性食品。

**しかし私たちが食べる物：** 全ての野菜と果物、米、卵不使用パスタと麺類、豆類、マッシュルーム、ナッツと種子類、穀物類。

**ヴィーガンミールを作るために：** 動物性油脂を植物油や植物性マーガリンに代え、スープやソースに野菜ストックを使い、全ての成分において動物性食品の有無を確認して創造的に考えます！

**私たちの要望に見合う食事を提供してくださるようお願い致します。**

ありがとうございます

# Kannada ಕನ್ನಡ

ದಯವಿಟ್ಟು ಇದನ್ನು ಓದಿ

**ನಾನು ಒಬ್ಬ ವೇಗನ್ / ನಾವು ವೇಗನ್ ಆಹಾರಾಭ್ಯಾಸವನ್ನು ರೂಢಿಸಿಕೊಂಡವರು**

ವೇಗನ್ ಆಹಾರಾಭ್ಯಾಸವನ್ನು ರೂಢಿಸಿಕೊಂಡವರು ಯಾವುದೇ ಪ್ರಾಣಿಜನ್ಯ ಪದಾರ್ಥವನ್ನು ಬಳಸದ ಸಸ್ಯಾಹಾರಿಗಳು.

**ಆದ್ದರಿಂದ ನಾವು ಇಂತಹ ಆಹಾರಗಳನ್ನು ಸೇವಿಸುವುದಿಲ್ಲ:** ಮಾಂಸ, ಕೋಳಿ (ಕೋಳಿಮರಿ, ಹೇಂಟೆ, ಹುಂಜಗಳು ಸೇರಿದಂತೆ), ಮೀನು, ಚಿಪ್ಪುಮೀನು, ಅಥವಾ ಯಾವುದೇ ಇತರೆ ಪ್ರಾಣಿಗಳ ಉತ್ಪನ್ನಗಳು, ಉದಾಹರಣೆಗಾಗಿ, ಮೊಟ್ಟೆಗಳು, ಹಾಲು ಅಥವಾ ಯಾವುದೇ ಡ್ಯೆರಿ ಉತ್ಪನ್ನಗಳು, ಜೇನುತುಪ್ಪ ಅಥವಾ ಜೆಲೆಟಿನ್.

**ಆದರೆ ನಾವು ಇವುಗಳನ್ನು ಸೇವಿಸುತ್ತೇವೆ:** ಎಲ್ಲಾ ತರಕಾರಿಗಳು ಮತ್ತು ಹಣ್ಣುಗಳು, ಅಕ್ಕಿ, ಮೊಟ್ಟೆ ರಹಿತ ಪಾಸ್ತಾ ಮತ್ತು ಶಾವಿಗೆಗಳು, ಬೀನ್ಸ್ ಬಗೆಗಳು, ಅಣಬೆಗಳು, ಕಾಳುಗಳು ಮತ್ತು ಬೀಜಗಳು, ಏಕದಳ ಧಾನ್ಯಗಳು ಮತ್ತು ದವಸ ಧಾನ್ಯಗಳು.

**ಒಂದು ವೇಗನ್ ಊಟವನ್ನು ತಯಾರಿಸಲು:** ಪ್ರಾಣಿಗಳ ಕೊಬ್ಬುಗಳ ಬದಲಿಗೆ ಸಸ್ಯಜನ್ಯ ಎಣ್ಣೆಗಳನ್ನು ಅಥವಾ ಸಸ್ಯಗಳ ಮಾರ್ಗರೀನ್ ಬಳಸಿ, ಸೂಪ್ ಮತ್ತು ಸಾಸ್ ಗಳಲ್ಲಿ ತರಕಾರಿಗಳ ಶೇಖರಣೆಗಳನ್ನು ಬಳಸಿ, ಎಲ್ಲಾ ಅಡಿಗೆ ಪದಾರ್ಥಗಳನ್ನು ಯಾವುದೇ ಪ್ರಾಣಿಗಳ ಉತ್ಪನ್ನಗಳಿಗಾಗಿ ಪರಿಶೀಲಿಸಿ, ಹಾಗೂ ಸೃಜನಾತ್ಮಕವಾಗಿ ಯೋಚಿಸಿರಿ!

**ನಮ್ಮ ಅವಶ್ಯಕತೆಗಳನ್ನು ಪೂರೈಸುವಂತಹ ಒಂದು ಊಟವನ್ನು ನೀವು ದಯವಿಟ್ಟು ಒದಗಿಸುವಿರಾ?**

ನಿಮಗೆ ತುಂಬಾ ಧನ್ಯವಾದಗಳು

# Khmer ខ្មែរ

សូមអានសារនេះ

**ខ្ញុំជាអ្នកតមសាច់/ពួកយើងជាអ្នកតមសាច់**

ក្នុងនាមជាអ្នកតមសាច់សត្វ ពួកយើងមិនបរិភោគអាហារណាដែលផលិតពីសាច់សត្វនោះទេ។

**យើងខ្ញុំមិនទទួលទាន៖** សាច់សត្វ
សាច់សត្វចិញ្ចឹមគ្រប់ប្រភេទ (រួមទាំងសាច់មាន់) ត្រីពពួកខ្យង ឬផលិតផលសាច់សត្វផ្សេងទៀតដូចជា ស៊ុតទឹកដោះគោ ឬផលិតផលប្រចាំថ្ងៃណាមួយដូចជាទឹកឃ្មុំ ឬចាហួយទេ។

**ប៉ុន្តែយើងខ្ញុំទទួលទាន៖** បន្លែនិផ្លែឈើគ្រប់ប្រភេទ បាយមីឬអាហារសរសៃគ្មានជាតិស៊ុត សណ្តែក ផ្សិត ដំណាប់និងគ្រាប់រុក្ខជាតិនិងធុញ្ញជាតិផ្សេងៗ។

**ដើម្បីរៀបចំអាហារសម្រាប់អ្នកតមសាច់សត្វដូចពួកយើង៖** សូមជំនួសខ្លាញ់សត្វដោយប្រើប្រេងធុញ្ញជាតិឬប៊ឺរធ្វើពីប្រេងរុក្ខជាតិ ត្រូវប្រើគ្រឿងផ្សំពីបន្លែសម្រាប់ធ្វើស៊ុបនឹងទឹកជ្រលក់ ត្រូវត្រួតពិនិត្យមើលធាតុផ្សំពីផលិតផលសាច់សត្វទាំងឡាយ និងត្រូវគិតដោយការច្នៃប្រឌិតខ្ពស់!

**តើលោកអ្នកអាចរៀបចំអាហារដែលអនុវត្តតាមលក្ខខណ្ឌតម្រូវខាងលើនេះបានឬទេ?**

សូមអរគុណយ៉ាងជ្រាលជ្រៅ

उपकार करून हें वाचचें

**हांव शाकाहारी/आमी शाकाहारी**

शाकाहारी जाल्ल्यान आमी जनावरां पसून मेळपी कांयच खायनात.

**म्हणटकच आमी खायनातः** मास, कक्कूट (कोमयेचें मास धरून), नुस्तें, तिसरी, खुबे, शिनाण्यो वा हेर जनावरांचें उत्पादन जशें तांतयां, दूद वा हेर डेअरी उत्पादनां, म्हौंव वा जिलेटीन.

**पूण आमी हें खाताता:** सगल्या तरेची भाजी आनी फळां, शी1त, तांतयां नाशिल्लो पास्ता आनी शेवयो, अळसांदे, अळमी, बियो आनी घट सालीचीं फळां, कड्डण आनी धान्य.

**शाकाहारी जेवण रांदूंकः** जनावराच्या चरबेच्या सुवातेर वनस्पती तेल वा मार्गारीन घेवचें, सूप आनी सॉसानीं भाजयेचो स्टॉक वापरचो, उत्पादनानीं जनावरांचे अंश नात हाची खात्री करूंक तातूंतले सगले द्रव्यघटक तपासचे आनी कल्पकतेन येवजुचें!

**उपकार करून, आमची गरज भागतली अशें जेवण तुमी उपलब्ध करशात?**

**देव बरें करूं**

# Korean 한국어

아래 내용을 읽어 주세요

저는 채식주의자입니다 / 우리는 채식주의자입니다

우리는 채식주의자이며 일체의 육류 음식을 먹지 않습니다.

먹지 않는 음식: 육류, 가금류(닭 포함), 어류, 조개류, 또는 달걀, 우유, 유제품, 꿀, 젤라틴 등 동물을 통해 생산된 식용 제품

먹을 수 있는 음식: 채소, 과일, 쌀, 달걀 성분이 없는 파스타, 국수, 콩, 버섯, 견과류, 시리얼, 곡류

비건 채식 요리를 만드는 방법: 동물성 유지방을 식물성 유지 또는 식물성 마가린으로 대체, 수프와 소스에 식물성 성분 사용, 육류 제품의 성분 확인, 입맛과 취향에 맞는 다양한 음식을 직접 요리.

우리가 섭취할 수 있는 음식을 제공해 주실 수 있나요?

감사합니다

## Lao ພາສາລາວ

ກະລຸນາອ່ານສິ່ງນີ້

**ຂ້ອຍແມ່ນຜູ້ກິນເຈ / ພວກເຮົາແມ່ນຜູ້ກິນເຈ**

ໃນຖານະທີ່ເປັນຜູ້ກິນເຈ ພວກເຮົາບໍ່ກິນສິ່ງໃດກໍ່ຕາມທີ່ເຮັດມາຈາກສັດ.

**ສະນັ້ນ ພວກເຮົາບໍ່ກິນ:** ມັງສາ(ຊີ້ນ), ສັດປີກ (ລວມທັງໄກ່), ປາ, ສັດນໍ້າມີເປືອກ, ຫຼື ຜະລິດຕະພັນສັດອື່ນໆ ເຊັ່ນ: ໄຂ່ໄກ່, ນໍ້ານົມ ຫຼື ທຸກຜະລິດຕະພັນທີ່ເຮັດຈາກນົມ, ນໍ້າເຜີ້ງ ຫຼື ວຸ້ນ.

**ແຕ່ພວກເຮົາກິນ:** ຜັກ ແລະ ໝາກໄມ້ກິນໝາກທຸກຊະນິດ, ເສັ້ນໝີ່ ແລະ ເສັ້ນເຝີທີ່ບໍ່ເຮັດຈາກໄຂ່ໄກ່, ໝາກຖົ່ວ, ເຫັດ, ເມັດຖົ່ວ ແລະ ເມັດພືດຕ່າງໆ, ຊີຣຽວ ແລະ ເມັດເຂົ້າ.

**ເພື່ອປຸງແຕ່ງອາຫານເຈ:** ໃຊ້ນໍ້າມັນພືດ ຫຼື ເນີຍທຽມເຮັດຈາກພືດແທນໄຂມັນສັດ, ໃຊ້ນໍ້າສະຕັອກຜັກໃນນໍ້າແກງ ແລະ ແຈ່ວຕ່າງໆ, ກວດສອບສ່ວນປະສົມທັງໝົດວ່າມີຜະລິດຕະພັນສັດໃດໆບໍ່ ແລະ ຄິດຢ່າງສ້າງສັນ!

**ຂໍຄວາມກະລຸນາແດ່ທ້ອນ, ຈັດຫາອາຫານທີ່ກົງກັບຄວາມຕ້ອງການຂອງພວກເຮົາໃຫ້ແນ່ໄດ້ບໍ?**

**ຂໍຂອບໃຈຫຼາຍໆ**

# Latvian  Latviešu valodā

LŪDZAM IZLASĪT

**Es esmu vegāns(-e) / Mēs esam vegāni**

Mēs esam vegāni, tāpēc neēdam jebkādus dzīvnieku izcelsmes produktus.

**Mēs neēdam:** gaļu, mājputnus (tai skaitā vistu), zivis, gliemjus un visus citus dzīvnieku izcelsmes produktus tādus kā olas, piens un visi piena produkti, medus un želatīns.

**Mēs ēdam:** visus dārzeņus un augļus, rīsus, pastu un nūdeles, kuru sastāvā nav olu, pupas, sēnes, riekstus un sēklas, graudaugus un graudus.

**Vegānā ēdiena pagatavošana:** dzīvnieku taukus aizvietojiet ar augu eļļu vai augu margarīnu, zupās un mērcēs izmantojiet dārzeņu buljonu, pārbaudiet, vai sastāvā nav dzīvnieku izcelsmes produktu, un esiet radoši!

**Vai jūs varētu pasniegt ēdienu, kas atbilst mūsu prasībām?**

LIELS PALDIES!

PRAŠAU PERSKAITYTI

**Aš esu veganas / Mes esame veganai**

Kadangi esame veganai, nevalgome gyvūninės kilmės produktų.

**Taigi, nevalgome** mėsos, paukštienos (įskaitant vištieną), žuvies, vėžiagyvių ar kitų gyvūninės kilmės produktų, tokių kaip kiaušiniai, pienas ar kiti pieno produktai, taip pat nevartojame medaus ar želatinos.

**Bet mes valgome** visas daržoves ir vaisius, ryžius, makaronus, pagamintus be kiaušinių, pupeles, grybus, riešutus, sėklas, javus ir grūdus.

**Gaminant veganų patiekalus** pakeiskite gyvulinius riebalus augaliniu aliejumi arba augaliniu margarinu, vartokite daržovių sultinį verdant sriubas ir padažus, patikrinkite visus ingredientus, ar nėra jokių gyvūninės kilmės produktų ir mąstykite kūrybiškai!

**Ar galėtumėte paruošti maistą, atitinkantį mūsų reikalavimus?**

LABAI JUMS AČIŪ

VAKIO AZAFADY

**Mpifadyhenaaho/Mpifadyhenaizahay**

Amin'nymahaolonampifadyhenaanaydiatsymihinanasakafoavyamin'nybibyizahay.

**Nohoizany, izahaydiatsymihinana:** hena,vorona (aoanatin'izanynyakoho), trondro, hazan-dranomasina, nasakafohafaavyamin'nybiby toy nyatody, ronono, naireovokatrahafa azo avyamin'nyronono, arynytantely.

**Kanefakosa, izahaydiamihinana:** nylegiomasynyvoankazorehetra, vary, patytsynampiasanaatody, voamaina, olatra, voasynykarazanavoarehetra.

**Rahahikarakarasakafo ho an'nympifadyhena dia:** soloymenaka azo avyamin'nyzava-manirynymenakaavyamin'nybibyrehetra, mampiasafanatsaranasakafosysaosytsymisyhena, hamarinotsaraavokoanysingarehetraaoanatin'nysakafosaomisyzavatraavyamin'nybiby, aryfaranydiamahaizamamorona!

**Mbaazonareoataoveazafadynymikarakarasakafomifanarakaamin'ireofangatahanayireo?**

MAKASITRAKA INDRINDRA

# Malay Bahasa melayu

SILA BACA

## Saya adalah vegan / Kami adalah vegan

Sebagai vegan kami tidak makan apa-apa yang berasal dari haiwan.

**Oleh itu, kami tidak makan:** daging , poltri (termasuk ayam), ikan, kerang-kerangan, atau apa-apa produk haiwan yang lain seperti telur, susu atau produk tenusu, madu atau gelatin.

**Tetapi kami makan:** semua sayur-sayuran dan buah-buahan, nasi, pasta bebas-telur dan mi, sayuran kacang, cendawan, kacang dan benih, bijiran dan butiran.

**Untuk membuat makanan vegan:** gantikan lemak haiwan dengan minyak sayur atau mentega sayur, gunakan stok sayur dalam sup dan sos, periksa semua bahan-bahan jika terdapat produk haiwan, dan berfikirlah secara kreatif !

**Bolehkah anda sediakan satu hidangan yang dapat memenuhi keperluan kami?**

TERIMA KASIH BANYAK

# മലയാളം

ദയവായി ഇത് വായിക്കുക

**ഞാൻ ഒരു സസ്യാഹാരിയാണ് / ഞങ്ങൾ സസ്യാഹാരികളാണ്.**

സസ്യാഹാരികൾ എന്ന നിലയ്ക്ക് ഞങ്ങൾ മൃഗ സ്രോതസ്സിൽ നിന്നുള്ള ഒന്നും കഴിക്കാറില്ല.

**ആയതിനാൽ ഞങ്ങൾ ഇവ കഴിക്കാറില്ല:** ഇറച്ചി, പൗൾട്രി (കോഴിയിറച്ചി ഉൾപ്പെടെ), മത്സ്യം, ഷെൽഫിഷ്, അല്ലെങ്കിൽ മുട്ട, പാൽ അല്ലെങ്കിൽ പാൽ ഉല്പന്നങ്ങൾ, തേൻ അല്ലെങ്കിൽ ജെലാറ്റിൻ തുടങ്ങിയ മറ്റേത് മൃഗ ഉല്പന്നവും.

**എന്നാൽ ഞങ്ങൾ ഇവ കഴിക്കും:** എല്ലാ പച്ചക്കറികളും പഴങ്ങളും, ചോറ്, മുട്ട ചേർക്കാത്ത പാസ്തയും നൂഡിൽസും, ബീൻസ്, കൂണുകൾ, അിവർഗ്ഗങ്ങളും കുരുക്കളും, പയറുവർഗ്ഗങ്ങൾ, ധാന്യങ്ങൾ.

**ഒരു സസ്യാഹാര ഭക്ഷണം തയ്യാറാക്കുന്നതിന്:** മൃഗക്കൊഴുപ്പിന് പകരം സസ്യ എണ്ണ അല്ലെങ്കിൽ സസ്യ മാർഗരൈൻ ഉപയോഗിക്കുക, സൂപ്പുകളിലും സോസുകളിലും സസ്യ സ്റ്റോക്ക് ഉപയോഗിക്കുക, മൃഗ ഉല്പന്നങ്ങൾ അടങ്ങിയിട്ടുോ എന്നറിയുന്നതിന് എല്ലാ ചേരുവകളും പരിശോധിക്കുക, ക്രിയാത്മകമായി ചിന്തിക്കുക!

**ദയവായി, ഞങ്ങളുടെ ആവശ്യകതകൾ പാലിക്കുന്ന ഒരു ഭക്ഷണം ലഭ്യമാക്കാൻ നിങ്ങൾക്കാവുമോ?**

**വളരെയധികം നന്ദി**

JEKK JOGĦĠBOK AQRA DAN

**Jiena vegan / Aħna vegans**

Bħala vegans aħna ma nieklu xejn li joriġina mill-annimali.

**B'hekk ma niklux:** laħam, tjur (inkluż tiġieġ), ħut, frott tal-baħar bil-qoxra, jew kwalunkwe prodott ieħor li ġej mill-annimali bħal bajd, ħalib jew prodotti tal-ħalib, għasel jew ġelatina.

**Iżda nieklu:** il-ħxejjex kollha u l-frott, ross, għaġin mingħajr bajd u noodles, fażola, faqqiegħ, ġewż u żrieragħ, ċereali u qamħ.

**Biex tagħmel ikla vegan:** issostitwixxi l-grass tal-annimali b'żejt veġetali jew marġerina veġetali, uża stokk tal-ħaxix f'sopop u zlazi, iċċekkja l-ingredjenti kollha għal kwalunkwe prodott li ġej mill-annimali, u aħseb b'mod kreattiv!

**Jekk jogħġbok tista' tipprovdi ikla li tissodisfa l-bżonnijiet tagħna?**

GRAZZI ĦAFNA

Marathi मराठी

कृपया हे वाचा

मी वीगन आहे / आम्ही वीगन्स आहोत

वीगन असल्यामुळे आम्ही प्राणिज असलेले काहीही खात नाही.

म्हणून आम्ही खात नाही: मांस, पोल्ट्री (चिकनसह), मासे, शेलफिश, किंवा अंडी, दूध किंवा दुग्धजन्य पदार्थ, मध किंवा जिलेटिनसारखे इतर कोणतेही प्राणिज पदार्थ.

पण आम्ही खातो: सर्व भाज्या आणि फळे, तांदूळ, अंडी-विरहित पास्ता आणि नूडल्स, बीन्स (शेंगा), मश्रूम, नट्स (सुका मेवा) आणि बिया, कडधान्ये आणि धान्ये.

वेगन जेवण बनविण्यासाठी: प्राण्यांच्या चरबीऐवजी वनस्पतीजन्य तेल किंवा वनस्पतीजन्य मार्गारिन वापरा, सूप्स आणि सॉसमध्ये भाज्यांचा स्टॉक वापरा, कोणत्याही प्राणिज उत्पादनांचे सर्व घटक तपासा, आणि नाविन्यपूर्णतेने विचार करा!

कृपया, आमच्या गरजा भागविणारे जेवण आपण पुरवू शकता काय?

आपले खूप खूप आभार

Mongolian **Монгол**

ҮҮНИЙГ УНШ

**Би мах иддэггүй хүн/ Бид мах иддэггүй хүн**

Мах иддэггүй хүний хувьд бид амьтны гаралтай юу ч иддэггүй.

**Тиймээс бид иддэггүй:** мах, тэжээвэр шувуу (тахиаг оруулна), загас, нялцгай биетэн эсвэл өндөг, сүү, ямар нэг сүүн бүтээгдэхүүн, зөгийн бал, царцмаг зэрэг аливаа бусад амьтны гаралтай бүтээгдэхүүн.

**Гэхдээ бид иддэг:** бүх төрлийн хүнсний ногоо, жимс, цагаан будаа, өндөггүй паста, гоймон, вандуй, мөөг, самар, үр, амуу тариа, үр тариа.

**Мах иддэггүй хүний хоолыг хийх:** Амьтны өөх тосыг хүнсний ногооны тос эвэл хүнсний ногооны маргарин тосоор орлуулах, шөл болон сүмсэнд хүнсний ногооны түүхий эдийг ашиглах, аливаа амьтны бүтээгдэхүүний бүх найрлагыг шалгах, бүтээлчээр сэтгэх!

**Бидний шаардлагыг хангах хоолоор хангаж болохсон болов уу?**

**МАШ ИХ БАЯРЛАЛАА**

# Nepali नेपाली

कृपया यसलाई पढ्नुहोस्

म भेगान हो/हामी भेगान हौं

भेगानको रूपमा हामी जनावरबाट उत्पति हुने कुनै पनि कुरा खादैनौं ।

**त्यसैले हामी निम्न कुरा खादैनौं:** मासु, कुखुरा लगायत कुनै पनि पक्षी, माछा, कवच-प्राणी, वा अन्डा, दूध, दूधबाट बनेका उत्पादनहरू, मह वा जिलेटिन जस्ता जीवजन्तु, पक्षी र माछाबाट निकालिने कुनै पनि वस्तु ।

**तर हामी निम्न कुराहरू खान्छौं:** सबै तरकारी तथा फलफूलहरू, भात, अन्डा नहालिएको पस्ता तथा चाउचाउ, गेडागुडी, च्याउ, नरिवल, बदाम, ओखर जस्ता फल तथा बीजहरू, अन्न तथा दानाहरू ।

**भेगान भोजन बनाउनको लागि:** जनावरबाट आएका घ्यु, बोसोलाई प्रतिस्थापित गरेर वनस्पति तेल वा वनस्पति मार्जरिन प्रयोग गर्नुहोस्, सुप तथा ससेजहरूमा तरकारीहरूबाट बनेका सरसामानहरू हाल्नुहोस्, सबै मरमसलाहरूमा कुनै जीवजन्तुको उत्पादन छ कि भनेर जाँच गर्नुहोस्, र रचनात्मक रूपमा सोच्नुहोस् !

**कृपया के तपाईं हामो आवश्यकताहरू पूरा गर्ने भोजन उपलब्ध गराउन सक्नुहुन्छ ?**

**तपाईंलाई धेरै-धेरै धन्यवाद !**

## Norwegian Norsk

VENNLIGST LES DETTE

**Jeg er en veganer / Vi er veganere**

Som veganere spiser vi ingenting som har animalsk opprinnelse.

**Så vi spiser ikke:** kjøtt, fjærfe (inkludert kylling), fisk, skalldyr, eller andre animalske produkter som egg, melk eller andre melkeprodukter, honning, eller gelatin.

**Men vi spiser:** alle typer grønnsaker og frukt, ris, pasta og nudler uten egg, bønner, sopp, nøtter og frø, cerealer og korn.

**Å lage en veganerrett:** erstatt animalsk fett med vegetabilsk olje eller vegetabilsk margarin, bruk grønnsaksbuljong i supper og sauser, sjekk alle ingrediensene for animalske produkter, og tenk kreativt!

**Kunne dere vennligst sørge for et måltid som passer til våre behov?**

TUSEN TAKK

## Persian

## فارسی

لطفاً این را بخوانید

**من یک وگان(گیاه خوار) هستم / ما وگانها(گیاهخواران) هستیم**

به عنوان یک وگان ما هیچ چیزی را با منشاء حیوانی مصرف نمی کنیم.

**بنابراین آنچه را که ما نمیخوریم:** گوشت، ماکیان (از جمله مرغ)، ماهی، صدف، یا هر محصول دیگر حیوانی مانند تخم مرغ، شیر و یا هرنوع فرآورده های لبنی، عسل یا ژلاتین.

**اما آنچه را که ما میخوریم:** تمام میوه ها و سبزیجات، برنج، ماکارونی و رشته فرنگی بدون تخم مرغ، لوبیا، قارچها، آجیل و دانه ها، غلات و حبوبات.

**تهیهٔ یک وعده غذای وگان:** جایگزینی چربی حیوانی با روغن نباتی یا مارگارین گیاهی، استفاده از سبزیجات در سوپ و سس، بررسی تمام مواد تشکیل دهنده برای هر گونه محصولات حیوانی، وذهن خلاقانه!

**لطفا، آیا می توانید غذایی را که مطابق با نیازهای ما است فراهم نمائید؟**

**خیلی ممنون**

# Polish Polski

PROSIMY, PRZECZYTAJ TO

**Jestem weganinem/Jesteśmy weganami**

Jako weganie nie spożywamy żadnych produktów pochodzenia zwierzęcego.

**Nie jemy zatem:** mięsa, drobiu (w tym kurczaka), ryb, skorupiaków oraz innych produktów pochodzenia zwierzęcego, tj. jajek, mleka oraz innego nabiału, miodu czy żelatyny.

**Jemy jednak:** wszystkie warzywa i owoce, ryż, makarony bezjajeczne, kluski, fasole, grzyby, orzechy i nasiona, płatki owsiane i zboża.

**Aby przyrządzić wegański posiłek:** zastąp tłuszcz zwierzęcy olejem roślinnym lub margaryną roślinną, w zupach i sosach używaj bulionu warzywnego, sprawdzaj listę składników pod kątem produktów pochodzenia zwierzęcego i myśl kreatywnie!

**Czy mógłbyś przyrządzić posiłek, który spełnia nasze wymagania?**

BARDZO DZIĘKUJEMY!

## Portuguese Português

POR FAVOR LEIA ISTO

**Sou vegano / Somos veganos**

Como veganos, não comemos nada de origem animal.

**Assim, não comemos:** carnes, aves (incluindo frango), peixe, marisco, nem qualquer outro produto de origem animal, como ovos, leite ou produtos lácteos, mel ou gelatina.

**Mas sim comemos:** todos os vegetais e frutas, arroz, massa sem ovo e macarrões, feijões, cogumelos, nozes e sementes, cereais e grãos.

**Para fazer uma refeição vegana:** substitua a gordura animal por óleo vegetal ou margarina vegetal, use caldo de legumes em sopas e molhos, verifique que os ingredientes não contêm produtos de origem animal, e pense de forma criativa!

**Pode fornecer uma refeição que se adapte às nossas necessidades?**

MUITO OBRIGADO

ਇਸਨੂੰ ਪੜ੍ਹਣ ਦੀ ਕ੍ਰਿਪਾ ਕਰੋ ਜੀ

**ਮੈਂ / ਅਸੀਂ ਵੈਸ਼ਨੂੰ (ਵੀਗਨ) ਹਾਂ।**

ਵੈਸ਼ਨੂੰ ਹੋਣ ਨਾਤੇ ਅਸੀਂ ਜਾਨਵਰਾਂ ਤੋਂ ਬਣੀ ਕੋਈ ਚੀਜ਼ ਨਹੀਂ ਖਾਂਦੇ।

**ਇਸ ਕਰਕੇ ਅਸੀਂ ਇਹ ਕੁੱਝ ਨਹੀਂ ਖਾਂਦੇ:** ਮਾਸ, (ਚੂਚਿਆਂ ਸਮੇਤ) ਪੰਛੀਆਂ ਦਾ ਮਾਸ, ਮੱਛੀ, ਸ਼ੈਲਫਿੱਸ਼, ਜਾਂ ਜਾਨਵਰਾਂ ਤੋਂ ਬਣੀਆਂ ਹੋਰ ਚੀਜ਼ਾਂ ਜਿਵੇਂ ਕਿ ਅੰਡੇ, ਦੁੱਧ ਜਾਂ ਡੇਅਰੀ ਉਤਪਾਦ, ਸ਼ਹਿਦ ਜਾਂ ਜਿਲੇਟਿਨ (ਸਰੇਸ਼)।

**ਪਰ ਅਸੀਂ ਇਹ ਕੁੱਝ ਖਾ ਲੈਂਦੇ ਹਾਂ:** ਸਭ ਸਬਜ਼ੀਆਂ ਅਤੇ ਫਲ, ਚੌਲ੍ਹ, ਅੰਡਾ ਰਹਿਤ ਪਾਸਤਾ ਅਤੇ ਨੂਡਲਜ, ਬੀਨਜ, ਖੁੰਭਾਂ, ਗਿਰੀਆਂ ਅਤੇ ਬੀਜ, ਸੀਰੀਅਲ ਅਤੇ ਦਾਣੇ।

**ਵੈਸ਼ਨੂੰ ਭੋਜਨ ਬਨਾਉਣ ਵਾਸਤੇ:** ਜਾਨਵਰਾਂ ਦੀ ਚਰਬੀ ਦੀ ਥਾਂ ਵੈਜੀਟੇਬਲ (ਸਬਜ਼ੀਆਂ ਦੇ) ਤੇਲ ਜਾਂ ਮਾਰਜਰੀਨ ਦੀ ਵਰਤੋਂ ਕਰੋ ਜੀ, ਸੂਪ ਅਤੇ ਸੋਸਾਂ ਵਿਚ ਵੈਜੀਟੇਬਲ ਸਟੌਕ ਵਰਤੋ, ਸਾਰੀ ਸਾਮੱਗ੍ਰੀ ਨੂੰ ਜਾਨਵਰੀ ਉਤਪਾਦਾਂ ਵਾਸਤੇ ਚੈਕ ਕਰੋ ਅਤੇ ਰਚਨਾਤਮਕ ਸੋਚ ਅਪਣਾਓ ਜੀ।

**ਕੀ ਤੁਸੀਂ ਕ੍ਰਿਪਾ ਕਰਕੇ ਸਾਡੀਆਂ ਲੋੜਾਂ ਦੀ ਪੂਰਤੀ ਕਰਨ ਵਾਲਾ ਭੋਜਨ ਮੁਹੱਈਆ ਕਰ ਸਕਦੇ ਹੋ ਜੀ?**

**ਆਪ ਜੀ ਦਾ ਬਹੁਤ ਬਹੁਤ ਧੰਨਵਾਦ**

VĂ RUGĂM SĂ CITIȚI ACEASTA

**Sunt vegan / Suntem vegani**

Ca vegani, nu mâncăm nimic care este de origine animală.

**Prin urmare nu mâncăm:** carne, carne de pasăre (inclusiv pui), pește, crustacee sau orice alte produse de origine animală cum ar fi ouă, lapte sau alte produse lactate, miere sau gelatină.

**Dar mâncăm:** toate fructele și legumele, orez, paste și tăieței care nu conțin ou, fasole, ciuperci, nuci și semințe, cereale și grâne.

**Pentru a prepara o masă vegană:** înlocuiți grăsimea animală cu ulei vegetal sau margarină vegetală, folosiți supă vegetală în ciorbe și sosuri, verificați că niciun ingredient nu conține produse de origine animală și gândiți creativ!

**Va rog, puteți pune la dispoziție o masă care să răspundă cerințelor noastre?**

VĂ MULȚUMESC FOARTE MULT

Russian **Русский**

ПОЖАЛУЙСТА, ПРОЧИТАЙ ЭТО

**Я веган / Мы веганы**

Будучи веганами, мы ничего не едим того, что является продуктом  животного происхождения.

**Значит мы не едим:** мясо, мясо домашней птицы (в том числе курицу), рыбу, морепродукты животного просихождения или любой другой продукт животного происхождения, такие как: яйца, молоко или какие-либо другие молочные продукты, мед или желатин.

**Но мы едим:** все овощи и фрукты, рис, макаронные изделия и лапшу, не содержащиеяйца, бобы, грибы, орехи и семечки, хлопья и зерна.

**Приготовление веганского блюда:** замени животный жир на растительное масло или растительный маргарин, используй овощной бульон для супов и соусов, проверяй все ингредиентылюбых продуктов животного происхождения и размышляй творчески!

**Пожалуйста, можешь ли ты приготовить блюдо, учитывая наши требования?**

**БОЛЬШОЕ ТЕБЕ СПАСИБО!**

MOLIMO PROČITAJTE OVO

**Ja sam vegan / Mi svo vegani**

Kao vegani mi ne jedemo ništa što je životinjskog porekla.

**Tako mi ne jedemo:** meso, živinu (uključujući piletinu), ribu, školjke, ili bilo koji drugi životinjski proizvod kao što su jaja, mleko ili neki drugi mlečni proizvod, med ili želatin..

**Ali mi jedemo:** svako povrće i voće, pirinač, pastu bez jaja i knedle, pasulj, pečurke, orahe i semenke, cerealije i žitarice.

**Da napravite vegansko jelo:** zamenite životinjske masti sa biljnim uljem ili biljnim margarinom, koristite kocku od povrća u supama i sosevima, proverite sve sastojke da li sadrže bilo koji životinjski proizvod i mislite kreativno.

**Molimo, da li možete obezbediti jelo koje odgovora našim zahtevima?**

HVALA VAM MNOGO

NDAPOTA VERENGAI IZVI

**Ndinodya muriwo chete / Tinodya muriwo chete**

Sevanhu vanodya muriwo chete hatidye chipi zvacho chinobva mumhuka.

**Saka hatidye:** nyama, chizarume (zvichisanganisira huku), hove, sherufishi, kana zvimwewo zvinobva mumhuka zvakaita semazai, mukaka kana zvipi zvazvo zvinogadzirwa nemukaka, huchi kana namo yegeratini.

**Asi tinodya:** miriwo yose nemichero, mupunga, pasita nemanudhuru zvisina kugadzirwa nemazai, bhinzi, hohwa, nzungu nemhodzi, masirieri nemumera.

**Kubika kudya kwemuriwo chete:** shandisa mafuta emuriwo kana majarini emuriwo panzvimbo pemafuta emhuka, shandisa muto wemuriwo musupu nesosi, ongorora zvinoshandiswa kubika zvose kuti hazvina zvinhu zvinobva mumhuka, uye iva nehusikisiki!

**Ndapota, munogona kutipa chikafu chinoenderana nezvatinotarisira here?**

TATENDA CHAIZVO

# Sinhalese සිංහල

කරුණාකර මෙය කියවන්න

**මම මස් මාළු නොකන්නෙකි / අපි මස් මාළු නොකන අය වෙමු**

මස් මාළු නොකන අය ලෙස, අපි සතුන්ගෙන් ලබා ගත් කිසිම දෙයක් නොකමු.

**අපි නොකන දේ නම්:** මස්, (කුකුළු මස් ඇතුළුව) කුකුළු ගණයේ ඒවා, මාළු, සිප්පි බෙල්ලන්, හෝ බිත්තර, කිරි හෝ යම් කිරි ආශ්‍රිත නිෂ්පාදන, මීපැණි හෝ ජෙලටින් වැනි අනෙකුත් යම් සතත්ව නිෂ්පාදන.

**නමුත් අපි කන ඒවා නම්:** සියලුම එළවළු සහ පලතුරු, හාල්, බිත්තර රහිත පැස්ටා සහා නූඩ්ල්ස්, බෝංචි වර්ග, හතු, බීජ වර්ග සහ ධාන්‍ය වර්ග.

**මස් මාළු රහිත ආහාර සෑදී සඳහා:** සතත්ව තෙල් වෙනුවෙන් එළවළු තෙල් හෝ එළවළු මාගරීන් භාවිත කරන්න, සූප් සහ සෝස් වර්ග සඳහා එළවළු නිෂ්පාදන භාවිත කරන්න, සතත්ව නිෂ්පාදන සහිත සියලුම දේ පරීක්ෂා කර බලන්න, නිර්මාණශීලී ලෙස කල්පනා කරන්න!

**කරුණාකර අපගේ අවශ්‍යතා සපුරන ආහාර වේලක් ඔබට සැපයිය හැකිද?**

**ඔබට අපගේ ස්තූතිය**

PROSÍM, PREČÍTAJTE SI NASLADOVNÉ

**Som vegán(-ka)/Sme vegáni**

Ako vegáni nejeme nič, čo má živočíšny pôvod.

**To znamená, že nejeme:** mäso, hydinu (vrátane kuracieho mäsa), ryby, mäkkýše, ani žiadne iné produkty živočíšneho pôvodu, ako sú vajcia, mlieko či mliečne výrobky, med a želatína.

**Ale jeme:** všetky druhy zeleniny a ovocia, ryžu, bezvaječné cestoviny a halušky, fazuľu, hríby, orechy a semená, cereálie a obilniny.

**Pri príprave vegánskeho pokrmu:** živočíšny tuk nahraďte rastlinným olejom alebo rastlinným margarínom, do polievok a omáčok použite zeleninový vývar, všetky prísady skontrolujte, či nie sú živočíšneho pôvodu, a buďte kreatívni!

**Môžete nám, prosím, poskytnúť jedlo podľa našich požiadaviek?**

ĎAKUJEME

# Slovenian Slovensko

PROSIMO PREBERITE

**Sem vegan(-ka)/Smo vegani**

Vegani ne jemo ničesar, kar je živalskega izvora.

**Ne jemo torej:** mesa, perutnine (vključno s piščancem), rib, lupinarjev ali katerih koli drugih živalskih izdelkov, kot so jajca, mleko ali drugi mlečni izdelki, med ali želatina.

**Jemo pa:** vso zelenjavo in sadje, riž, testenine in rezance, ki ne vsebujejo jajc, fižol, gobe, oreščke in semena, kosmiče in žitarice.

**Za pripravo veganskega obroka:** namesto živalske masti uporabljajte rastlinsko olje ali rastlinsko margarino, v juhah in omakah uporabljajte zelenjavno jušno osnovo, zagotovite, da se v sestavinah ne nahajajo živalski proizvodi in bodite kreativni!

**Prosimo, če lahko zagotovite obrok, ki izpolnjuje naše zahteve?**

NAJLEPŠA HVALA

FADLAN AKHRI TAN

**Waxaan ahey fijiteeriyan/Waxaanu nahay fijiteeriyan**

Dadka fijiteeriyanka ahi ma cunaan wax kasta oo ka sameysan xawayaan.

**Sidaas darted ma cuno:** hilibka, hilibka shimbiraha (marka lagu darro digaaga), kaluun, xayawaanka qolofleyda ah, ama wax kale oo ka soo jeeda xawayaan sida beedka, caanaha ama waxyaalaha caanaha ka sameysan, malabka ama jelaatiinta.

**Laakiin waxaanu cunaa:** dhamaan khudaarta iyo khudrada, bariiska, baastada iyo noodleska aanu beedku ku jirin, digirta, likaha/mashroomiska, lawska iyo siidhka, siiriyalka iyo badaka

**Si aad u sameyso cuntada fijiteeriyanka:** Marku hore ku badel subaga xoolaha ka khudaarta, suugada iyo maraqa u isticmaal maraqa ka sameysan khudaarta, ka fiiri dhamaan waxyaalaha ay ka sameysantey inaanay ku jirin waxyaalaha ka soo jeeda xawayaanka, una fikir si maskaxeysan!

**Fadlan, miyaad sameyn kartaa cunto buuxineysa baahidayada?**

AAD AYAAD U MAHADSAN TAHAY

# Spanish Español

POR FAVOR, LEAN ESTO

**Soy vegano/ Somos veganos**

Como veganos, no comemos nada de origen animal.

**Por ello, no comemos:** carne, aves de corral (incluido el pollo), pescado, marisco ni ningún otro producto animal, como huevos, leche o cualesquiera productos lácteos, miel ni gelatina.

**Pero sí comemos:** todo tipo de verduras y frutas, arroz, pasta sin huevo, fideos sin huevo, alubias (judías, frijoles, porotos, caraotas) y otras legumbres (garbanzos, lentejas, guisantes, habas, etc.), champiñones, frutos secos y semillas, cereales y granos.

**Para hacer una comida vegana:** sustituyan la grasa animal por aceite vegetal o margarina vegetal, usen caldo de verduras en sopas y salsas, comprueben que los ingredientes no incluyan productos animales, ¡y piensen de manera creativa!

**Por favor, ¿pueden ofrecernos una comida que cumpla estas condiciones ?s**

MUCHAS GRACIAS

TAFADHALI SOMA HAPA

**Sili nyama / Hatuli nyama**

Kwa kuwa hatuli nyama hatuli chochote chenye asili ya nyama.

**Kwa hiyo hatuli:** nyama, ndege (pamoja na kuku), samaki, magamba ya samaki, au bidhaa zozote za wanyama kama mayai, maziwa au bidhaa za maziwa, asali au gelatin.

**Lakini tunakula:** mboga zote, na matunda, mchele, mayai yasiyo na pasta na nudo, maharage, uyoga, njugu na mbegu, sirio na nafaka.

**Kutengeneza chakula cha asiyekula nyama:** weka mafuta ya mimea badala ya ya wanyama au siagi za mboga, tumia stoku ya mboga kwenye supu na mchuzi, angalia viungo vyote kama vina bidhaa za wanyama, nafikiria kwa makini!

**Tafadhali, unaweza kutupatia chakula kinachokidhi mahitaji yetu?**

ASANTE SANA

VÄNLIGEN LÄS DETTA

**Jag är vegan / Vi är veganer**

Som vegan äter vi inte några livsmedel med animaliskt ursprung.

**Vi äter alltså inte:** kött, fågel (inklusive kyckling), fisk, skaldjur, eller någon annan typ av animalisk produkt såsom ägg, mjölk eller några mjölkprodukter, honung eller gelatin.

**Vi äter dock:** alla grönsaker och frukter, ris, äggfri pasta och nudlar, bönor, svamp, nötter och frön, spannmål och korn.

**Hur man tillagar en vegansk måltid:** byt ut animaliskt fett mot vegetabilisk olja eller vegetabiliskt margarin, använd grönsaksbuljong i soppor och såser, kontrollera att ingredienserna inte innehåller några animaliska produkter och tänk kreativt!

**Var snäll och tillaga en måltid som uppfyller dessa krav.**

TACK SÅ MYCKET

# Tagalog Pilipino

MANGYARING BASAHIN ITO

**Ako ay isang vegan/ Mga vegan kami**

Bilang isang vegan hindi kami kumakain ng kahit ano na nanggagaling sa hayop.

**Kaya hindi namin kinakain ang:** karne, mga ibon, (kabilang ang manok), isda, kabibi, o anumang iba pang produkto ng hayop tulad ng itlog, gatas o anumang produkto ng gatas, pulot, o gulaman.

**Ngunit kinakain namin ang:** lahat ng gulay at prutas, kanin, walang itlog na pasta at mga pansit, mga butil, kabuti, mga mani at buto, mga siryal at haspe.

**Upang gumawa ng pagkaing vegan:** palitan ang taba ng hayop sa langis ng halaman o margarin na gulay, gumamit ng sabaw ng gulay sa mga sopas at sarsa, suriin ang lahat ng mga sangkap para sa anumang mga produkto ng hayop, at maging malikhain sa pag-iisip!

**Mangyari po, maaari ka bang magbigay ng pagkain na makakatugon sa aming mga kinakailangan?**

MARAMING SALAMAT PO

*தயவு செய்து இதனை வாசியுங்கள்*

***நான் தாவர உணவு உண்பவர் / நாம் தாவர உணவு உண்போர்***

*தாவர உணவு உண்போர் என்ற வகையில் நாம் விலங்குகளிலிருந்து உற்பத்தியாகும் எதனையும் உண்பதில்லை.*

***எனவே நாம் உண்ணாதவை:*** *இறைச்சி, (கோழியிறைச்சி உட்பட) பறவையிறைச்சி, மீன், சிப்பி, அல்லது முட்டை, பால் அல்லது எந்தவொரு பாற் பொருளும், தேன் அல்லது ஜெலட்டின் போன்ற விலங்குத் தயாரிப்பு எதுவும்.*

***ஆனால் நாம் உண்பவை:*** *மரக்கறி வகைகள், பழங்கள், அரிசி, முட்டையில்லாத பஸ்டாவும் நூடில்ஸும், அவரை வகைகள், காளான், பருப்பு வகைகளும் கொட்டைகளும், கூலங்கள், தானியங்கள் ஆகிய அனைத்தும்.*

***தாவர உணவொன்றைச் சமைப்பதற்கு:*** *விலங்குக் கொழுப்புக்குப் பதிலாக மரக்கறி எண்ணெய்யை அல்லது மரக்கறி மாகரீனைப் பயன்படுத்துங்கள், சூப் வகைகளிலும் சோஸ் வகைகளிலும் தாவரப் பொருட்களைப் பயன்படுத்துங்கள், விலங்குறப்பத்தி உள்ளதா என்று எல்லா உணவுப் பொருட்களையும் சோதித்துப் பாருங்கள், ஆக்கபூர்வமாகச் சிந்தியுங்கள்!*

***எங்களது தேவைகளை அடைந்து கொள்ளும் ஒருணவை நீங்கள் எங்களுக்கு வழங்குவீர்களா?***

***மிக்க நன்றி***

# Telugu **తెలుగు**

దయచేసి ఇది చదవండి

**నేను శాకాహారిని / మేం శాకాహారులం**

ఒక శాకాహారిగా మేం జంతు మూలంగా వచ్చే ఏ ఆహారాన్నీ తినం.

**కాబట్టి మేం వీటిని తినము:** మాంసం, పౌల్ట్రీ(చికెన్‌తో సహా), చేపలు, గుల్లచేపలు, లేదా గుడ్లు, పాలు లాంటి ఇతర జంతు ఉత్పత్తులు లేదా మరేపైనా పాల ఉత్పత్తులు, తేనె లేదా జిలాటిన్.

**కానీ మేం వీటిని తింటాము:** అన్ని కూరగాయలు మరియు పండ్లు, అన్నం, గుడ్డు-వేయని పాస్తా మరియు నూడుల్స్, బీన్స్, పుట్టగొడుగులు, పప్పులు, తృణధాన్యాలు, ధాన్యాలు.

**శాకాహార భోజనం వండటానికి:** జంతు కొవ్వుకు బదులుగా వెజిటబుల్ ఆయిల్(ఉదా:వేరుశెనగనూనె) లేదా వెజిటబుల్ మార్గరిన్ వాడండి, సూపులు, సాసుల్లో వెజిటబుల్ స్టాక్(కూరగాయలతో చేసే గుజ్జు)ను వాడండి, అన్ని వంట పదార్థాల్లో ఏపైనా జంతు సంబంధిత ఉత్పత్తులు ఉన్నాయేమో చూడండి, అలాగే సృజనాత్మకంగా ఆలోచించండి!

**ప్లీస్, మీరు మా అవసరాలకు సరిపోయే భోజనాన్ని అందించగలరా?**

**థాంక్యూ వెరీ మచ్**

โปรดอ่านข้อความต่อไปนี้

**ฉันทานอาหารมังสวิรัติ / เราทานอาหารมังสวิรัติ**

ในฐานะที่เป็นมังสวิรัติเราไม่กินอาหารที่ปรุงมาจากสัตว์

**เราไม่ทานอาหารประเภท:** เนื้อ, เป็ดไก่ (รวมถึงสัตว์ปีก), ปลา, หอย, หรือผลิตภัณฑ์จากสัตว์ต่าง ๆ เช่น ไข่, นมหรือผลิตภัณฑ์จากนม, น้ำผึ้ง หรือ เจลาติน

**เราทานอาหารประเภท:** ผักและผลไม้, ข้าว, พาสต้าและก๋วยเตี๋ยวที่ไม่มีส่วนผสมของไข่, ถั่ว, เห็ด, เมล็ดพืช และธัญพืช

**ในการปรุงอาหารมังสวิรัติ:** ให้ใช้น้ำมันพืชหรือเนยเทียมแทนไขมันสัตว์ ใช้ผักในการทำน้ำซุปและซอส ตรวจสอบส่วนผสมทั้งหมดว่าไม่มีผลิตภัณฑ์ใด ๆ จากสัตว์ และคิดอย่างสร้างสรรค์!

**คุณจะกรุณาจัดเตรียมอาหารให้ตรงกับความต้องการของเราได้หรือไม่**

**ขอบคุณมาก**

# Tibetan

# བོད་ཡིག

འདི་གློག་རྟགས་གནང་།

**ང་ལྷི་སྐན་ཡིན། / ང་ཚོ་ལྷི་སྐན་ཡིན།**

ལྷི་སྐྱན་ཡིན་པའི་རྐྱེན་གྱིས་ང་ཚོས་སེམས་ཅན་ཐོན་ཁུངས་ཅི་ཡང་བཟའ་ཡི་མེད།

**དེས་ན་ང་ཚོས་གང་མི་བཟའ་བ་ནི།:** ཤ་དང་ཁྱིམ་བྱ། (བྱ་ཤ་འཚུད་པ་ཡིན།) དེ་བཞིན་ཉ་དང་ཉ་སོག ཡང་ན། སེམས་ཅན་གྱི་ཐོན་ཁུངས་ཅི་རིགས། དཔེར་ན། སྒོ་ང་། འོ་མའམ་འོ་མའི་ཐོན་རྫས་སྦྲང་རྩི་འམ་སྤྱིན་ཁུ་ལྟ་བུ།

**འོན་ཏེ་ང་ཚོས་གང་བཟའ་ཡི་ཡོད་ཞེ་ན།** སྔོ་ཚལ་དང་ཤིང་ཏོག་ཆ་ཚང་། དེ་བཞིན་འབྲས། སྒྲོང་མེད་ཕུག་པ། རྒྱ་སྲན། ཤ་མོ། སྟར་ག་དང་འབྲུ་རིགས། ལྷི་སྐན་ཁ་ཟས་བཟོ་བར། སེམས་ཅན་གྱི་ཚིལ་ཞག་ཚབ་ཏུ་སྔོ་ཚལ་གྱི་སྣུམ་མམ་སྔོ་ཚལ་མར་རྫས་སྤྱོད་ཅིང་། ཐང་དང་སྤྱོད་སྨན་ནང་སྔོ་ཚལ་གྱི་རྩི་ཤིང་བེད་སྤྱོད་བྱ། ཟས་ཀྱི་རྫས་ཆའི་ནང་དུ་སེམས་ཅན་གྱི་ཐོན་ཁུངས་གང་ཡང་མེད་པའི་ཞིབ་བཤེར་བྱེད་པའི་ཐོག། བསམ་བློ་རྒྱ་བསྐྱེད་གྱིས།

སྐུ་མཁྱེན།

ཁྱེད་ཀྱིས་ང་ཚོའི་དགོས་མཁོ་དང་མཐུན་པའི་ཟས་ཞིག་མཁོ་སྤྲོད་བྱེད་ཐུབ་པས།

ཐུགས་རྗེ་ཆེ།

በይዝአም እዚ መልእኽቲ የንብብዎ

**አነ ኣትክልቲ ተመጋቢ እየ / ንሕና ኣትክልቲ ተመገብቲ ኢና**

ኣትክልቲ ተጠቀምቲ ስለዝኾና ዝኾነ ይኹን ናይ እንስሳት ተዋፅኦ ኣይንምገብን፡፡

**ስለዚ እንምገቦም ምግብታት ዝሰዕቡ እዮም**- ስጋ፣ ንስጋን እንቁቁሓን ዝኾኑ ልማድያ የዕዋፋ /ደርሆ ሐዊስካ/ ዓሳ፣ ጠንካራ ሽፋን ዘለዎ ከምኡውን ዝኾነ ንምግብነት ዝኸውን ናይ እንስሳት ውፅኢተት እዚ ማለት እንቁላሊሕ፣ ፀባ ዝኾነ ዓይነት ናይ ፀባ ተዋፅኦ፣ መዓር፣ ዘፅግብ ምግብን

**ኮዩኑ ግን ዝሰዕቡ ምግብታት ውን ንምገብ ኢና**-ኩሎም ዓይነታት ኣትክልቲ ፈረምረ፣ ሩዝ፣ ብእንቁላሊሕ ዘይተሰረሐ ፖስታን ድልኽ፣ ዓተር፣ ቕንጢሽራ ፣ ናይ ቕብአት አኽልታት፣ ጥረመረ ናይ እኽሊ ዘርኢ

**ንአትክልቲ ተመግብቲ ምግቢ ስለምስራሕ**-ናይ እንስሳት ዘይቲ ብኣትክልቲ ዘይቲ ወይ ናይ ኣትክልቲ ማረጋሪን ብምትካእ ብሸረባ፣ መረቕ፣ ውሽቀዊ ኣትክልቲ ውፅኢታት ንምጥቃም፣ ናይ እንስሳት ተዋፅኦ ምህረታት ምንባሮም ውን ተፋትሽ ከካየድ ብምግባር ዝሐስ ሓዱሽ ሐሳብ የቕረቡ ።

**በይዝኦም ኣብ ስዕሊ ዝገለፅናዮም አገደስቲ መላከዕታት ብምምላኢ ምግቢ ሰከናዱእልና ይኽእሉ ዶ?**

ንትሕብብሮም አዚና ነመስግን!

# Turkish Türkçe

LÜTFEN BUNU OKUYUN

**Ben veganım. / Biz veganız.**

Biz veganlar hayvansal olan hiçbir şeyi yemiyoruz.

**Yani şunları yemiyoruz:** et, (tavuk dahil) kümes hayvanları, balık, kabuklu deniz hayvanları, yumurta, süt veya süt ürünleri, bal ya da jelatin gibi hayvansal ürünler.

**Ama şunları yiyoruz:** bütün sebzeler ve meyveler, pirinç, içinde yumurta olmayan makarna ve erişte, baklagiller, mantarlar, kuruyemiş, hububat ve tahıllar.

**Vegan yemeği yapmak için:** hayvansal yağ yerine sıvı ya da katı bitkisel margarin kullanın, çorba ve soslarda sebze bulyonları kullanın, herhangi bir hayvani malzeme kullanılıp kullanılmadığını kontrol edin, ve yaratıcı olmaya çalışın!

**Bu kriterlere uygun yemek çıkarabilir misiniz?**

ÇOK TEŞEKKÜRLER

БУДЬ ЛАСКА, ПРОЧИТАЙТЕ ЦЕ

**Я веган / Ми вегани**

Бувши веганами, ми не їмо нічого тваринного походження.

**Так що ми не їмо:** м'ясо, птицю (в тому числі куряче м'ясо), рибу, молюски або інши тваринні продукти як яйця, молоко або будь-які молочні продукти, мед або желатин.

**Але ми їмо:** всі овочі і фрукти, рис, макарони і локшину, які не містять яєць, квасолю, гриби, горіхи і насіння, крупи та зерна.

**Щоб зробити веганське харчування:** потрібно замінити жири тваринного походження на рослинну олію або овочевий маргарин, використовувати овочевий бульйон в супах і соусах, перевірте всі інгредієнти для будь-яких продуктів тваринного походження вам потрібно мислити креативно!

**Будь ласка, ви можете забезпечити їжу, яка відповідає нашим вимогам?**

**ДУЖЕ ВАМ ДЯКУЄМО**

براہ مہربانی اسے پڑھیں

**میں ایک سبزی خور ہوں / ہم سبزی خور ہیں**

ایک سبزی خور کے طور پر ہم جانورں سے بننے والی کوئی غذا نہیں کھاتے ہیں۔

**تو ہم نہیں کھاتے ہیں:** گوشت، پولٹری (بشمول چکن)، مچھلی، شیل فش، یا کوئی بھی دیگر جانوروں سے بنی مصنوعات جیسا کہ انڈے، دودھ یا کوئی بھی دودھ کی مصنوعات، شہد یا جلیٹن۔

**لیکن ہم کھاتے ہیں:** تمام سبزیاں اور پھل، چاول، انڈے سے پاک پاستا اور نوڈلز، پھلیاں، مشرومز، گریاں اور بیج، دلیے اور اناج۔

**ایک نباتاتی کھانا بنانے کے لئے:** جانوروں ماخذ کی چکنائی کو نباتاتی تیل یا نباتاتی مارجرین سے بدل دیں، سوپ اور ساسز یا چٹنیوں میں سبزی اسٹاک استعمال کریں، کسی بھی جانور کی مصنوعات کے تمام اجزاء کی پڑتال کریں، تخلیقی انداز میں !سوچیں

**براہ مہربانی کیا آپ ایسا کھانا مہیا کر سکتے ہیں جو ہماری ضروریات پر پورا اترتا ہے؟**

بہت بہت شکریہ

## Vietnamese **Tiếng việt**

XIN VUI LÒNG ĐỌC THÔNG ĐIỆP NÀY

**Tôi là người ăn chay / Chúng toi là những người ăn chay**

Là người ăn chay chúng tôi không ăn những thực phẩm có nguồn gốc từ động vật.

**Vì thế chúng tôi không ăn:** thịt, gia cầm (kể cả gà), cá, tôm cua, hay bất cứ sản phẩm động vật nào khác như trứng, sữa hoặc bất cứ sản phẩm nào từ sữa, mật ong hoặc keo động vật.

**Nhưng chúng tôi ăn:** tất cả các loại rau củ quả, gạo, mì ống và mì dẹt không chứa thành phần trứng, đậu, nấm, hạnh nhân và các loại hạt, ngũ cốc và hạt thô.

**Để chế biến một bữa ăn chay:** thay thế mỡ động vật bằng dầu thực vật hay bơ thực vật, sử dụng nguyên vật liệu thực vật trong các món súp và nước xốt, kiểm tra tất cả các thành phần để loại bỏ bất cứ sản phẩm nào có nguồn gốc từ động vật, và tư duy một cách sáng tạo!

**Bạn có thể chế biến được một bữa ăn đáp ứng được các yêu cầu của chúng tôi không?**

**CẢM ƠN BẠN RẤT NHIỀU**

## Welsh Cymraeg

DARLLENWCH HWN OS GWELWCH YN DDA

**Figan dw i / Figaniaid ydym ni**

Gan ein bod yn figaniaid, nid ydym yn bwyta unrhyw beth o gynnyrch gan anifeiliaid.

**Felly nid ydym yn bwyta:** cig, dofednod (gan gynnwys cyw iâr), pysgod, pysgod cregyn, neu unrhyw gynnyrch gan anifeiliaid megis wyau, llefrith neu unrhyw gynnyrch llaeth, mêl neu gelatin.

**Ond rydym yn bwyta:** pob llysieuyn a ffrwyth, reis, pasta a nwdls yn rhydd o wyau, ffa, madarch, cnau a hadau, grawn a grawnfwydydd.

**I wneud pryd o fwyd figanaidd:** cyfnewidiwch fraster anifeiliaid am olew llysieuol neu fargarîn llysieuol, defnyddiwch stoc lysieuol mewn cawliau a sawsiau, gwiriwch bob cynhwysyn am gynnyrch gan anifeiliaid, a meddyliwch yn greadigol!

**Allwch chi ddarparu pryd sy'n ateb ein gofynion, os gwelwch yn dda?**

DIOLCH YN FAWR IAWN

SICELA UFUNDE OKU

**Ngiyivegeni / Siyizivegeni**

Njengeevegeni asikudli okwesilwane.

**Asidli oku:** inyama, okweenkuku (kubandakanya nenkuku), intlanzi, sisnenke okanye namiphi na into yesilwane njengamaqanda, libisi okanye nantonina yederi, amakhekheba okanye ijelathi.

**Yaye sidla:** imifino yonke neethelo, iraysi, ipasta engenaqanda nenodlisi, ziibhontshisi, inkowankowane, iinatsi, iisidi, iisireli neenhlamvu.

**Ukze wenze ukudla kweevegeni:** endaweni yefethi zeelwane sebenzisa ezemfino okanye imajarini yemfino, sebenzisa iisosi neesobho zemifino, khangela zonke iithako ngezinto zesilwane, bese uyacingiaisa!

**Siyacela, ungakutsho ukutsha okusifaneleyo?**

SIBULELA GQITHA

JỌ̀WỌ̀ KA ÈYÍ

**Èmi ni vegan / Àwa ni vegans**

Gẹ́gẹ́ bii Vegan àwa kìí jẹ ohunkóhun ti ó bá jẹ́ ẹran.

**Wàyí o, a kì í jẹ:** ẹran, ohun-ọ̀sìn abìyẹ́ (tí ó fi mọ́ adìyẹ), ẹja, ìgbín, tàbí ohunkóhun tí à ń rí lára ẹranko bí ẹyin, mílíìkì, tàbí èyíkéyìí ohun-èlò tí à ń pèsè láti àra ẹranko, oyin tàbí gẹlatín-nì.

**Ṣùgbọ́n a máa ń jẹ́:** gbogbo ẹ̀fọ́ àti èso, ìrẹsì, pasta aláìlẹ́yin, àti nódùùsì, ẹwà, olú, obì àti èso, sìrîìlì àti ọka bàbà.

**Láti pèsè oúnjẹ vegan:** lo orórò ẹfọ́ dípò òróró ẹran tàbí bọ́tà, lo àwọn ohun-èlò ẹ̀fọ́ nínú ọbẹ̀ àtí ọbẹ́ ata, wo àwọn èròjà dáàdáà láti mọ bóyá ó ni èròjà ẹranko nínú kí o sì wá ọgbọ́n mìíràn dá!

**Jọ̀wọ́, ǹjẹ́ o lè pèsè oúnjẹ tí ó wà ní ìbámu pẹlú àwọn ìlànà**

**O ṢE PÚPỌ̀**

SICELA UFUNDE LOKHU

**Ngiyivegeni / Singamavegeni**

Njengamavegeni asidli noma yini evela esilwaneni.

**Ngakho asiyidli:** inyama, okwezinkukhu (kuhlanganise nekukhu), inhlanzi, umnenke, noma imiphi imikhiqizo evela esilwaneni njengamaqanda, ubisi noma imiphi imikhiqizo yederi, uju noma ijelathini.

**Kodwa sidla:** yonke imifino mezithelo, irayisi, iphasta engemaqanda namanodulisi, ubhontshisi, amakhowe, amakinati, namasidi, amasireli nokusanhlamvu.

**Ukuze wenze ukudla kwamavegeni:** esikhundleni samafutha esilwane faka awemifino noma imajarini yemifino, sebenzisa amasobho emifino namasosi, hlola zonke izithako ngayo yonke imikhiqizo yesilwane, bese ucabanga ngokuhlakanipha!

**Siyacela, ungakunikeza ukudla okuhlangabezana nezimfuneko zethu?**

SIBONGA KAKHULU

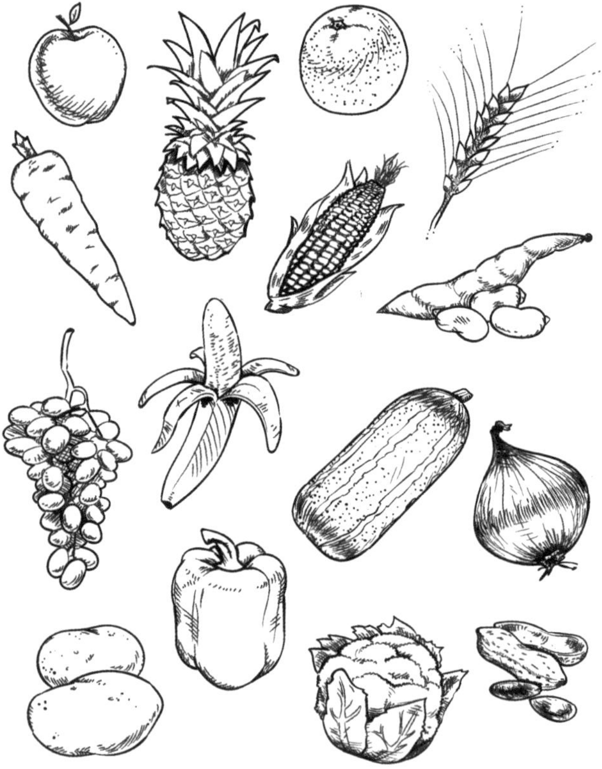

Vegan Airline Meal Code

# VGML

**Vegan airline meal code** **Код бортового питания для веганов**

纯素食者航空餐饮代码

ভিগান এয়ারলাইনের খাদ্যনীতি **Spezialmenü-Buchungscode**

**Código para refeição vegan das companhias aéreas**

**Code IATA repas végétalien** वीगन एयरलाइन भोजन सुचकांक

**رمز وجبات طعام خطوط الطيران للغذاء النباتي**
**(الخال من جميع مشتقات الحيوانات بما في ذلك البيض ومشتقات الحليب).**

**Código comida vegana línea aérea** **Kodo manĝa vegana aerlinia**

ヴィーガン（完全菜食）の航空機内食記号

# Index

# Index

# Index

# Index

# Index

# Additional Resources

## Useful Websites

http://www.vegansociety.com
http://www.happycow.net
http://www.vegetarianguides.co.uk/index.shtml
http://www.todovegano.com
http://www.vrg.org/travel/

## The Vegan Trademark

Look out for the above logo on products and at restaurants as this logo means that the ingredients have been checked by The Vegan Society and you can be sure that they are free from animal ingredients and free from animal testing.

If you would like more information on The Vegan Society or the benefits of a vegan diet then please contact us:
www.vegansociety.com
info@vegansociety.com

The Vegan Society
Donald Watson House
21 Hylton Street
Hockley
Birmingham
B18 6HJ

# Notes

# Notes